THE QUEST
FOR
COSMIC JUSTICE

Thomas Sowell

A TOUCHSTONE BOOK
PUBLISHED BY SIMON & SCHUSTER
NEW YORK   LONDON   TORONTO   SYDNEY

TOUCHSTONE
Rockefeller Center
1230 Avenue of the Americas
New York, NY 10020

First Touchstone Edition 2002
TOUCHSTONE and colophon are trademarks
of Simon & Schuster, Inc.

For information about special discounts for bulk purchases,
please contact Simon & Schuster Special Sales:
1-800-456-6798 or business@simonandschuster.com

Designed by Brady McNamara
Printed in the United States of America

10   9   8   7

The Library of Congress has cataloged
the Free Press edition as follows:
Sowell, Thomas, 1930–
        The quest for cosmic justice / Thomas Sowell.
            p.   cm.
        Includes bibliographical references and index.
        1. Social justice.   2. Equality.   I. Title.
    HM671.S68   1999   99-31470   CIP
    303.3'72—dc21

ISBN-13: 978-0-684-86462-4
ISBN-10:   0-684-86462-2
ISBN-13: 978-0-684-86463-1 (Pbk)
ISBN-10:   0-684-86463-0 (Pbk)

Contents

Preface

General principles, such as "justice" or "equality," are often passionately invoked in the course of arguing about the issues of the day, but such terms usually go undefined and unexamined. Often much more could be gained by scrutinizing what we ourselves mean by such notions than by trying to convince or overwhelm others. If we understood what we were really saying, in many cases we might not say it or, if we did, we might have a better chance of making our reasons understood by those who disagree with us.

The heady rush of rhetoric and visions are the stuff of everyday politics and everyday media discussion. That makes it all the more important that, at some point, we step back and examine what it all means underneath the froth or glitter. This book is an attempt to do that.

The ideas discussed here took shape over a long period of time. The title essay evolved out of a paper I gave in St. Gallen, Switzerland, in 1982 on "Trade-Offs and Social Justice." By 1984, it was recast and elaborated at great length in another paper called "Social Justice Reconsidered," which was circulated to various people around the country, including Milton Friedman and Mancur Olson. Professor Friedman's typically incisive criticisms were followed by the opinion that "it is well worth the effort required to put it in shape." Professor Olson's comments were likewise critical and perhaps not quite as encouraging. I too understood the difficulties of that draft, which was academic and radically different in form from what appears in this book.

Over the years, "Social Justice Reconsidered" evolved into "The Quest for Cosmic Justice," completely recast yet again, but still not finished a decade later. Nor was it certain that it ever would be finished, given the various other projects I was involved in. However, in the spring of 1996, some particularly sophomoric remarks by one of my Stanford colleagues not only provoked my anger but also convinced me that there was a real need to untangle the kind of confusions that could lead any sensible adult to say the things he had said—and which all too many other people were saying. I went home and immediately resumed work on the essay on cosmic justice, writing it now for the general public, rather than for an academic audience.

By the autumn of 1996, the new version was completed and I presented "The Quest for Cosmic Justice" as a lecture in New Zealand. Much to my pleasant surprise, large excerpts from it were published in the country's leading newspapers. This press coverage, as well as the enthusiastic reception of the talk by a non-academic audience, convinced me that this was something that the general public would understand—perhaps more readily than some academics who are locked into the intellectual fashions of the day.

The other essays in this book also evolved over a period of years and within a similar framework of thought that now gives them a collective coherence, even though they were written to stand alone individually. The central ideas in "Visions of War and Peace" first appeared in an article of that title that I published in 1987 in the British journal *Encounter.* The current and much briefer version is now a section in the essay "The Tyranny of Visions."

The generosity of Milton Friedman and the late Mancur Olson in criticizing the earlier, academically oriented paper of mine is much appreciated, but of course they share no responsibility for any shortcomings of the present, very different essay, aimed at a more general audience. In a truly just world, I would also have to acknowledge my debt to my colleague whose sloppy thinking galvanized me into action. However, I shall not do so by name, in deference to collegiality and to the libel laws in a litigious society.

THOMAS SOWELL
Rose and Milton Friedman Senior Fellow
Hoover Institution
Stanford University

I

The Quest for Cosmic Justice

. . . justice, if only we knew what it was.

—Socrates

One of the few subjects on which we all seem to agree is the need for justice. But our agreement is only *seeming* because we mean such different things by the same word. Whatever moral principle each of us believes in, we call justice, so we are only talking in a circle when we say that we advocate justice, unless we specify just what conception of justice we have in mind. This is especially so today, when so many advocate what they call "social justice"—often with great passion, but with no definition. All justice is inherently social. Can someone on a desert island be either just or unjust?

INEQUALITIES AND INJUSTICES

If social justice can be distinguished from any other conception of justice, it is probably by its reaction against the great inequalities of income and wealth which we see all around us. But reactions against such inequalities are not limited to those who proclaim "social justice." It was not a radical writer, but free-market economist Milton Friedman, who referred to "gross inequities of income and wealth" which "offend most of us" and declared: "Few can fail to be moved by the contrast between the luxury enjoyed by some and the grinding poverty suffered by others."[1]

While such views have often been associated with the political left, many of the thinkers and writers identified as "conservative" have long expressed similar views, objecting not only to economic inequalities but also to extreme inequalities of power and respect. Two centuries ago, Adam Smith, the father of laissez-faire economics, deplored not only the callousness of the rich and powerful of his day, "who never look upon their inferiors as their fellow-creatures," but deplored also our "obsequiousness to our superiors" and the "foolish wonder and admiration" shown toward "the violence and injustice of great conquerors."[2]

While a few conservative writers here and there have tried to justify inequalities on grounds of "merit," most have not. The late Nobel Prize–winning economist and free-market champion Friedrich A. Hayek, for example, declared, "the manner in which the benefits and burdens are apportioned by the market mechanism would in many instances have to be regarded as very unjust *if* it were the result of a deliberate allocation to particular people." The only reason he did not regard it as unjust was because "the particulars of a spontaneous order cannot be just or unjust."[3] The absence of personal intention in a spontaneous order—a cosmos, as Hayek defined it[4]—means an absence of either justice or injustice. "Nature can be neither just nor unjust," he said. "Only if we mean to blame a personal creator does it make sense to describe it as unjust that somebody has been born with a physical defect, or been stricken with a disease, or has suffered the loss of a loved one."[5]

Others who share a similarly secular view are often driven to personify "society" in order to re-introduce concepts of moral responsibility and justice into the cosmos, seeking to rectify the tragic misfortunes of individuals and groups through collective action in the name of "social justice." Yet this collective action is not limited to correcting the consequences of *social* decisions or other collective social action, but extends to mitigating as well the misfortunes of the physically and mentally disabled, for example. In other words, it seeks to mitigate and make more just the undeserved misfortunes arising from the cosmos, as well as from society. It seeks to produce *cosmic* justice, going beyond strictly *social* justice, which becomes just one aspect of cosmic justice.

As the philosopher Thomas Nagel put it, "the range of possibilities or likely courses of life that are open to a given individual are limited to a considerable extent by his birth"—which includes not only the social class and home environment into which he happened to be born but also "his genetic endowment." This last, especially, is clearly not social. Yet "from a moral point of view," Professor Nagel said, "there is nothing wrong with the state tinkering with that distribution" of life chances, which distribution "does not have any moral sanctity."[6] Thus, in this view, to "provide equality of opportunity it is necessary to compensate in some way for the unequal starting points that people occupy."[7] The difference between Nagel and Hayek in this regard is not in their understanding of the painful inequalities that both recognize, but in their respective conceptions of justice.

Even those few writers who have tried to justify inequalities on merit grounds are nevertheless conceding that inequalities are things requiring justification. Virtually no one regards these inequalities as desirable in themselves. If the world had chanced to be more equal than it is, it is hard to see who would have had any grounds for complaint, much less just grounds.

Nor should we imagine that quantifiable economic differences or political and social inequalities exhaust the disabilities of the less fortunate. Affluent professional people have access to all sorts of sources of free knowledge and advice from highly educated and knowledgeable friends and relatives, and perhaps substantial financial aid in time of crisis from some of these same sources. They also tend to have greater access to those with political power, whether through direct contacts or through the simple fact of being able to make an articulate presentation in terms acceptable to political elites. Moreover, the fact that the affluent tend to have the air of knowledgeable people makes them less likely to become targets for many of the swindlers who prey on the ignorant and the poor.

Even in legitimate businesses, "the poor pay more," as the title of a book said some years ago, because it costs more to deliver goods and services to low-income, high-crime neighborhoods, where insurance and other costs are higher.[8] In short, statistical inequalities do not begin to exhaust the advantages of the advantaged or the disadvantages of the disadvantaged.

With people across virtually the entire ideological spectrum being offended by inequalities and their consequences, why do these inequalities persist? Why are we not all united in determination to put an end to them? Perhaps the most cogent explanation was that offered by Milton Friedman:

A society that puts equality—in the sense of equality of outcome—ahead of freedom will end up with neither equality nor freedom. The use of force to achieve equality will destroy freedom, and the force, introduced for good purposes, will end up in the hands of people who use it to promote their own interests.[9]

Whatever the validity of this argument—and one need only think of the horrors of Stalin, Mao, and Pol Pot to realize that painful possibilities are not mere fantasies—it rejects direct political equalization of economic results because the costs are judged to be too high. Still it finds no positive virtue in inequality. But what of those who do not reject the cost as too high? Do they simply have a different assessment of those costs and risks? Or do they proceed with little or no attention to that question?

A trivial example may illustrate some of the costs of correcting some kinds of inequalities and injustices. In San Francisco in 1996, a relative of one of the city's supervisors telephoned a pizza company to ask to have a pizza delivered to his home. He was told that the company did not deliver pizza where he lived, which happened to be in a high-crime neighborhood. Immediately there was an outburst of moral indignation. A law was passed, decreeing that anyone who makes deliveries to the public in any part of the city must make deliveries all over the city.

Here, in this simple example, we have all the elements of the quest for cosmic justice. Since most people are not criminals, even in a high-crime neighborhood, large numbers of innocent people have various additional costs imposed on them through no fault of their own—in this case, the cost of being unable to receive deliveries of food, furniture, packages, and other things that other people take for granted elsewhere. They are treated unequally. From a cosmic perspective, this is an injustice, in the sense that, if we were creating the universe from scratch, this is not something that most of us would choose to include in it.

However, unlike God at the dawn of Creation, we cannot simply say, "Let there be equality!" or "Let there be justice!" We must begin with the universe that we were born into and weigh the costs of making any specific change in it to achieve a specific end. We cannot simply "do something" whenever we are morally indignant, while disdaining to consider the costs entailed. In this case, the increased costs would include dead truck drivers. In American high-crime neighborhoods, the probability that a given young man living there will be killed is greater than the probability that a given American soldier would be killed in World War II. While the odds may not be as great for someone making deliveries there, they may also not be negligible. Nor should we ignore the possibility that an outsider may attract more attention and resentment, resulting in greater risks.

Once we begin to consider how many deliveries are worth how many dead truck drivers, we have abandoned the quest for cosmic justice and reduced our choices to the more human scale of weighing costs versus benefits. Across a wide spectrum of issues, the difference between seeking cosmic justice and seeking traditional justice depends on the extent to which costs are weighed. The enormous difference that this can make needs to be made explicit, so that we do not keep talking past one another on something as important as justice.

Cosmic justice is not simply a higher degree of traditional justice, it is a fundamentally different concept. Traditionally, justice or injustice is characteristic of a *process*. A defendant in a criminal case would be said to have received justice if the trial were conducted as it should be, under fair rules and with the judge and jury being impartial. After such a trial, it could be said that "justice was done"—regardless of whether the outcome was an acquittal or an execution. Conversely, if the trial were conducted in violation of the rules and with a judge or jury showing prejudice against the defendant, this would be considered an unfair or unjust trial—even if the prosecutor failed in the end to get enough jurors to vote to convict an innocent person. In short, traditional justice is about impartial processes rather than either results or prospects.

Similar conceptions of justice or fairness extend beyond the legal system. A "fair fight" is one in which both combatants observe the rules, regardless of whether that leads to a draw or to a one-sided beating. Applying the same rules of baseball to all meant that Mark McGwire hit 70 home runs while some other players hit less than 10. The "career open to talents" or "a level playing field" usually means that everyone plays by the same rules and is judged by the same standards. Again, if the process itself meets that standard, then no matter what the outcome, "you had your chance." But this is not what is meant by those people who speak of "social justice." In fact, rules and standards equally applicable to all are often deliberately set aside in pursuit of "social justice." Nor are such exceptions aberrations. The two concepts are mutually incompatible.

What "social justice" seeks to do is to eliminate undeserved disadvantages for selected groups. As in the San Francisco pizza delivery case, this is often done in disregard of the costs of this to other individuals or groups—or even to the requirements of society as a whole. When one considers a society such as Sri Lanka, where group preferences initiated in the 1950s led to decades of internal strife, escalating into bitter civil war with many atrocities, it is not purely fanciful to consider that other societies may become more polarized and contentious—to everyone's ultimate detriment—by similar schemes of preferential treatment for one segment of society. Intergroup relations in the United States, for example, have never been as good as they once were in Sri Lanka—nor, fortunately, are they as bad as they later became in Sri Lanka.

In its pursuit of justice for a segment of society, in disregard of the consequences for society as a whole, what is called "social justice" might more accurately be called *anti-social* justice, since what consistently gets ignored or dismissed are precisely the costs to society. Such a conception of justice seeks to correct, not only biased or discriminatory acts by individuals or by social institutions, but unmerited disadvantages in general, from whatever source they may arise. In American criminal trials, for example, before a murderer is sentenced, the law permits his unhappy childhood to be taken into account. Seldom is there any claim that the person murdered had anything to do with that presumptively unhappy childhood. In a notorious 1996 case in California, the victim was a twelve-year-old girl, who had not even been born when the murderer was supposedly going through his unhappy childhood. It is only from a cosmic perspective that his childhood had any bearing on the crime.

If punishment is meant to deter crime, whether by example or by putting existing criminals behind bars or in the graveyard, then mitigating that punishment in pursuit of cosmic justice presumably means reducing the deterrence and allowing more crime to take place at the expense of innocent people. At a more mundane level, the enormously increased amount of time required to ponder the imponderables of someone else's childhood (and related speculations) means that the criminal justice system as a whole operates more slowly and that other criminals are therefore walking the streets on bail while awaiting trial in an overloaded court system.

Prosecutors who should be moving on to other criminals after securing a murder conviction must instead spend additional time putting together a rebuttal to psychological speculation. Even if this speculation does not in the end affect the outcome in the case at hand, it affects other cases that are left in limbo while time and resources are devoted to rebutting unsubstantiated theories. A significant amount of the violent crimes committed in America is committed by career criminals who are walking the streets—and stalking the innocent—while awaiting trial. This too is one of the costs of the quest for cosmic justice.

Much, if not most, of the concerns billed as "social justice" revolve around economic and social inequalities among groups. But the general principles involved are essentially the same as in other examples of pursuing cosmic justice. These principles have been proclaimed by politicians and by philosophers, from the soapbox to the seminar room and in the highest judicial chambers. Such principles deserve closer scrutiny and sharper definition.

MEANINGS OF JUSTICE

Back in the 1960s, President Lyndon Johnson made one of the classic statements of the vision of cosmic justice:

> You do not take a man who, for years, has been hobbled by chains, liberate him, and bring him to the starting line of a race,

saying, "You are free to complete with all others," and still justly believe you have been completely fair.[10]

Professor John Rawls' celebrated treatise, *A Theory of Justice*, puts the case more generally. According to Rawls, "undeserved inequalities call for redress," in order to produce "genuine equality of opportunity."[11] This is "fair (as opposed to formal) equality of opportunity."[12] In other words, having everyone play by the same rules or be judged by the same standards is merely "formal" equality, in Professor Rawls' view, while truly "fair" equality of opportunity means providing everyone with equal prospects of success from equal individual efforts.

Note how the word "fair" has an entirely different meaning in this context. Cosmic justice is not about the rules of the game. It is about putting particular segments of society in the position that they would have been in but for some undeserved misfortune. This conception of fairness requires that third parties must wield the power to control outcomes, over-riding rules, standards, or the preferences of other people.

Such attitudes are found from college admissions offices to the highest courts in the land. Thus a long-time admissions director at Stanford University has said that she never required applicants to submit Achievement Test scores because "requiring such tests could unfairly penalize disadvantaged students in the college admissions process," since such students "through no fault of their own, often find themselves in high schools that provide inadequate preparation for the Achievement Tests."[13] *Through no fault of their own* — one of the key phrases in the quest for cosmic justice. Nor are such attitudes unique to Stanford. They are in fact common across the country.[14]

In short, all are not to be judged by the same rules or standards within the given process; pre-existing inequalities are to be counter-balanced. Note also that, once again, the quest for cosmic justice focusses on one segment of the population and disregards the interests of others who are not the immediate focus of discussion, but who nevertheless pay the price of the decisions made. After all, taxpayers and donors provide billions of dollars annually for the education of the next generation, but there is little or no sense of responsibility to them to maximize the productivity of the education they pay for, rather than engage in self-indulgent feel-goodism. Nor is there any concern for the effects on society as a whole in not putting educational resources where they will produce the largest return.

Since "undeserved inequalities" extend beyond prejudicial decisions made by others to encompass biological differences among individuals and groups—the fact that women are usually not as large or as physically strong as men, for example—and profound differences in the geographical settings in which whole races and nations have evolved culturally,[15] not to mention individual and group differences in child-rearing practices and moral values, cosmic justice requires—or assumes—vastly more knowledge than is necessary for traditional justice.

Requirements for Cosmic Justice

Implicit in much discussion of a need to rectify social inequities is the notion that some segments of society, through no fault of their own, lack things which others receive as windfall gains, through no virtue of their own. True as this may be, the knowledge required to sort this out intellectually, much less rectify it politically, is staggering and superhuman. Far from society being divided into those with a more or less standard package of benefits and others lacking those benefits, each individual may have both windfall advantages and windfall disadvantages, and the particular combination of windfall gains and losses varies enormously from individual to individual. Some are blessed with beauty but lacking in brains, some are wealthy but from an emotionally impoverished family, some have athletic prowess but little ability to get along with other human beings . . . and so on and on. Add to this the changing circumstances of each individual over a lifetime — with relative advantages and disadvantages changing with the passing years — and the difficulties of merely determining the net advantages increase exponentially.

As just one example, a young woman of unusual beauty may gain many things, both personal and material, from her looks, without having to develop other aspects of her mind and character. Yet when age begins to rob her of that beauty, she may be left much less able to cope than others who never had the benefit of her earlier windfall gain. The challenge of determining the net balance of numerous windfall advantages and disadvantages for one individual at one given time is sufficiently daunting. To attempt the same for whole broad-brush categories of people, each in differing stages of their individual life cycles, in a complex and changing society, suggests hubris.

Ironically, some find in the complexities of the world a reason to abandon fixed rules and standards, in favor of individual fine-tuning. For example, a book seeking to justify racial preferences in college admissions was titled *The Shape of the River* because of a conversation on a river boat:

"You've got to know the shape of the river perfectly. It is all there
is left to steer by on a very dark night . . ."

"Do you mean to say that I've got to know all the million tri-
fling variations of shape in the banks of this interminable river
as well as I know the shape of the hall at home?"

"On my honor, you've got to know them better."[16]

Can anyone seriously believe that college admissions officials
can know individual applicants that well? Only by equating
guesswork based on popular psychology and fashionable social
theories with actual knowledge. Any river boat which operated
that way would have run aground long ago.

Much of the quest for cosmic justice involves racial,
regional, religious, or other categories of people who are to be
restored to where they would be but for various disadvantages
they suffer from various sources. Yet each group tends to trail
the long shadow of its own cultural history, as well as reflecting
the consequences of external influences. The history of every
people is a product of innumerable cross-currents, whose tim-
ing and confluence can neither be predicted beforehand nor
always untangled afterward. There is no "standard" history that
everyone has or would have had "but for" peculiar circumstances of particular groups, whose circumstances can be "corrected" to conform to some norm. Unravelling all this in the
quest for cosmic justice is a much more staggering task than
seeking traditional justice.

To apply the same rules to everyone requires no prior knowledge of anyone's childhood, cultural heritage, philosophical (or
sexual) orientation, or the innumerable historical influences to

which he or his forebears may have been subjected. If there are any human beings capable of making such complex assessments, they cannot be numerous. Put differently, the dangers of errors increase exponentially when we presume to know so many things and the nature of their complex interactions. In particular, it is all too easy to be overwhelmed by clear and tragic historic injustices—and to glide easily from those injustices to a *cause-and-effect* explanation of contemporary problems. We know, of course, that causation and morality are two different things. Too often, however, we proceed as if we did not recognize this distinction.

In the United States, for example, many of the social problems of the contemporary black underclass are almost automatically attributed to "a legacy of slavery." The prevalence of fatherless families in the black ghettos, for example, has been widely explained by the lack of legally constituted families under slavery. But if one proceeds beyond plausibility and guilt to actually seek out the facts, an entirely different picture emerges.

A hundred years ago, when blacks were just one generation out of slavery, the rate of marriage in the black population of the United States was slightly *higher* than that of the white population. Most black children were raised in two-parent families, even during the era of slavery, and for generations thereafter. The catastrophic decline of the black nuclear family began, like so many other social catastrophes in the United States, during the decade of the 1960s. Prior to the 1960s, the difference in marriage rates between black and white males was never as great as 5 percentage points. Yet, today, that difference is greater than 20 percentage points—and widening, even though the nuclear family is also beginning to decline among white

Americans.[17] Whatever the explanation for these changes, it lies much closer to today than to the era of slavery, however disappointing that may be to those who prefer to see social issues as moral melodramas.

The tragic and monumental injustice of slavery has often been used as a causal explanation of other social phenomena, applying to both blacks and whites in the Southern United States, where slavery was concentrated—without any check of the facts or comparisons with other and more mundane explanations. The fact that there are large numbers of black Americans today who are not in the labor force has also been one of those things causally (and often rather casually) attributed to slavery. But again, if we go back a hundred years, we find that labor force participation rates among blacks were slightly *higher* than among whites—and remained so, on past the middle of the twentieth century.[18] If we want to know why this is no longer so, again we must look to events and trends much closer to our own time.

For the white population as well, many observers of nineteenth-century America saw striking social and economic differences between Southern whites and Northern whites—the Southerners having less education, poorer work habits, less entrepreneurship, more violence, and lower rates of invention, among other things. Even such astute observers as Alexis de Tocqueville attributed such differences to the adverse effects of slavery on the attitudes of Southern whites. Yet, if one traces back to Britain the ancestors of these Southerners, one finds the very same social patterns in these and other things, long before they crossed the Atlantic or saw the first black slave.

Migrations from Britain, like migrations from many other countries, were from highly specific places in the country of origin to highly specific places in the country of destination. Most of the people who settled in the colony of Massachusetts, for example, came from within a 60-mile radius of a town in East Anglia. Those who settled in the South came from different regions with very different cultural patterns. Moreover, the cultural contrasts between these people that many would later comment on in America had already been noted and commented on in Britain in earlier times, when these contrasts had nothing to do with slavery, which did not exist in Britain at that time.

We can all understand, in principle, that even a great historic evil does not automatically explain all other subsequent evils. But we often proceed in practice as if we did not understand that. Cancer can indeed be fatal, but it does not explain all fatalities, or even most fatalities.

The larger point here is how easy it is to go wrong, by huge margins, when presuming to take into account complex historical influences. The demands of cosmic justice vastly exceed those of traditional justice—and vastly exceed what human beings are likely to be capable of. The great U.S. Supreme Court justice Oliver Wendell Holmes said that there may be some people who are simply born clumsy, so that they may inadvertently injure themselves or others—for which, presumably, they will not be blamed when they stand before the courts of heaven. But, in the courts of man, they must be held to the same standards of accountability as everyone else. We do not have the omniscience to know who these particular people are or to what extent they were capable of taking extra precautions to guard against their own natural tendencies. In other words, human courts should not presume to dispense cosmic justice.

No small part of the legal shambles of the American criminal justice system since the 1960s, accompanied by skyrocketing rates of violent crime, resulted from attempts to seek cosmic justice in the courtrooms. In a series of U.S. Supreme Court decisions in the early 1960s, various restrictions were placed on the police in their arrest and interrogation of suspects in criminal cases, and in the search of their property. The rationales for these restrictions included the claim—undoubtedly true—that inexperienced and amateurish criminals, ignorant of the law, were more likely to make admissions that would later prove to be fatally damaging to their own legal defense, while sophisticated professional criminals and members of organized crime syndicates were far less likely to trap themselves in this way.

Clearly this is an injustice from some cosmic perspective— and correcting this inequity among criminals was explicitly the perspective of the Attorney General of the United States and of the Chief Justice of the Supreme Court at that time.[19] However, as in other instances of the quest for cosmic justice, the costs to third parties were largely disregarded, pretended not to exist, or dismissed with some such lofty phrase as "That is the price we pay for freedom." Presumably, the United States was not a free country until the 1960s.

A more recent *cause célèbre* of the American criminal justice system was the murder trial of former football star O. J. Simpson, which provoked widespread consternation, not only because of its "not guilty" verdict in the face of massive evidence to the contrary, but also because of the sheer length of time that the trial took. It was more than a year after the murder itself before the trial concluded, even though Simpson was arrested within days after the body of his former wife was discovered. Those who take on the daunting task of defending the current American criminal justice system were quick to claim that it was the defendant's wealth, celebrity, and race which made the trial so long, as well as the verdict so unexpected, thereby making the case too atypical to be part of a general indictment of the American criminal justice system. However, an even longer time elapsed in another contemporary murder case in which *none* of these factors was present, even though that suspect was likewise arrested not long after that crime.

Nearly three years elapsed between the murder of twelve-year-old Polly Klaas in 1993 and the sentencing of her murderer, Richard Allen Davis, in 1996—even though there was such evidence against the killer that there was not even a claim made by his defense attorney that Davis had not committed the crime. What could have taken so long then? Among other things, there were extended arguments over all sorts of legal technicalities—technicalities created not by legislation but by the judicial interpretations of appellate courts, seeking to remove ever more remote dangers of injustice by creating the greater injustice of crippling a society's ability to defend itself in even the clearest cases of unquestioned guilt.

"Merit" and Cosmic Justice

Related to cosmic justice is the seductive, misleading, and often pernicious concept of "merit," which is either explicit or implicit in much that is said by people in various parts of the philosophical spectrum.

A man born to ignorant, abusive, immoral, and drug-ridden parents may exhibit great personal merit in becoming nothing more than an honest and sober laborer who supports his family and raises his children to be decent and upright citizens—while another man, born to the greatest wealth and privilege and educated in the finest schools, may exhibit no greater personal merit in becoming a renowned scientist, scholar, or entrepreneur. Indeed, would most of us not rejoice more to see such a laborer win millions of dollars in a lottery than we would to see this scientist, scholar, or entrepreneur gain millions because of his proficiency in his chosen field? Have religious people not for centuries held out the hope that humble but decent people would someday receive a more transcendent reward in a better world after death? It does not matter that some leaders may have held out such hopes cynically, in order to reconcile people to their painful fate in this world, for such cynicism works only because it resonates with a feeling that is genuine in others.

For some, it is but a short step from wishing that personal merit were rewarded—here and now—to promoting policies designed either to do so or simply to redistribute wealth in general, on grounds that much or most of that wealth is unmerited by those who currently hold it. Tales about princes and paupers who were mistakenly switched at birth, or about servants living "downstairs" who have as much (or more) character as their wealthy employers living "upstairs," all resonate with the idea that many factors besides personal merit determine our economic and social fates. No doubt this belief is true to a very considerable extent, certainly to a greater extent than many of us would wish. But, again, the question is not what we would do if we were God on the first day of Creation or how we would judge souls if we were God on Judgment Day. The question is: What lies within our knowledge and control, given that we are only human, with all the severe limitations which that implies?

One of the many differences between human beings and God on Judgment Day is that God does not have to worry about what is going to happen the day after Judgment Day. Our decisions do not take place at the end of time, but rather in the midst of the on-going stream of time, so that what we do today affects how others will respond tomorrow and thereafter. History is full of examples of countries which made it difficult for individuals to acquire or retain great wealth in the marketplace—and which then found it difficult to attract or to hold the capital needed to raise the living standards of the masses.

Conversely, places where money is easily made, easily repatriated, and lightly taxed have made phenomenal economic progress, even when they have had pathetically few natural resources—Hong Kong as a British colony and Singapore as an independent city-state being classic examples. It is by no means clear that most of those who earned great wealth in Hong Kong or Singapore did so solely, or even primarily, as a result of personal merit. But to drive out or discourage their capital and entrepreneurship through confiscatory policies would be to sacrifice the standard of living of millions of others, in order to produce income and wealth distribution statistics pleasing to that small number of intellectuals who follow such things.

In short, two intractable obstacles stand in the way of rewarding merit: First and most fundamentally, we do not know how to do it. While we may be able to surmise from a few dramatic examples that personal merit need not correspond with reward, we have no generally applicable way to know how much of each individual's success or failure was due to such windfall gains as innate ability, a favorable upbringing, family wealth, or simply being in the right place at the right time, and how much was due to such personal merits as hard work and sacrifice. Moreover, even the latter virtues are often to some extent a consequence of upbringing. But even if we could somehow miraculously acquire the omniscience to know all these things and how they interact in complex ways, we would still be left with the fact that changing rewards today changes incentives tomorrow—not just for those benefitting from unmerited good fortune, but for millions of others in the same society.

Wishing to see a poor but meritorious man win a lottery is radically different from instituting government redistributive policies. A lottery creates no precedent, no system of legal entitlements, and no reason for millions of people to change their behavior in ways that may prove to be detrimental to society as a whole. Nor does a lottery require vast amounts of knowledge about individuals, since everyone knows that it is just a matter of luck. Private charity is likewise neither precedential nor a basis on which millions of people can depend for support for a changed lifestyle of avoiding work and living off others.

Merit justifications for income and wealth differences are also fundamentally different from productivity justifications, even though the two are often confused. Someone with an inborn knack for mathematics or music may be just as productive as someone who was born with lesser talents in these fields and who had to work very hard to achieve the same level of proficiency. However, we reward productivity rather than merit, for the perfectly valid reason that we know how to do it. Moreover, since rewards represent not merely retrospective judgments but prospective incentives as well, a society can become more productive by rewarding productivity, whether by encouraging some to work hard to achieve such productivity or by encouraging others to step forward to reveal and apply their existing productivity.

The incentive effects of rewarding productivity operate in other ways as well. While the existing practitioners in a given field may be adequately (or even excessively) rewarded for their performance level, there may nevertheless be a case to be made for raising salaries in a particular field, in order to attract a higher caliber of person, capable of a higher level of performance, than the current norm in that field. This argument might be made for school teachers but it applies even more so to politicians and judges. Yet people who are preoccupied with merit are highly susceptible to demagogues who denounce the idea of paying politicians, for example, more money that they clearly do not deserve, in view of their current dismal performances. To get beyond this demagoguery requires getting beyond the idea of considering pay solely from the standpoint of retrospective reward for merit and seeing it from the standpoint of prospective incentives for better performances from new people.

Pay for productivity, rather than merit, encourages better performances in yet another way. In a constantly developing economy, new and better ways of accomplishing various tasks mean that obsolescence is continually forcing older products and older methods of production out of the economy. In other words, equally meritorious people may receive very different rewards, simply because one group happens to be in a declining industry or using obsolete technology, while another happens to be in a rising industry or using advanced technology. These are not zero-sum games, however. Society as a whole has more prosperity when it is more productive. Put differently, the injustice of such unmerited rewards can be corrected only at the cost of creating an injustice to millions of others, who can become needlessly poorer, or fail to rise to the level of prosperity that existing technology and resources would permit.

An even more serious injustice can occur if government officials are given greater powers, in order to have them create "social justice," for once the powers have been given, they can be used to create despotism instead—as has happened in the French, Bolshevik, and other revolutions, for example.

Those who argue as to whether the poor are "deserving" or "undeserving" often argue past each other because they are not clear as to whether their respective frameworks are those of cosmic justice or traditional justice. Even the most degenerate member of the underclass may *in some cosmic sense* be said to be what he is because of circumstances—at least in the sense that he might have been raised in other ways that might have increased the likelihood of his becoming a decent human being.

Even if his brothers and sisters, raised under the same roof, turned out well, who can be certain that some other combination of circumstances—whether gentler treatment or stricter discipline—might not have turned him around before it was too late? But, from the standpoint of traditional justice, the question is entirely different: Failing to know specifically how particular individuals could have been prevented from becoming dangers to others, especially when their siblings came out of the same home with a sense of decency, are we better off to pretend to know how to fine-tune children's upbringing to this degree or instead to put individuals on notice that certain violations of other people's rights will subject the violators to an array of punishments?

Again, if we were creating our own cosmos, surely we would not wish to have in it some individuals so impervious to decent influences that they could turn out to be menaces to society and disgraces to their families. But, given that we must cope with a universe that was not tailor-made to our desires, the question becomes whether disgrace itself may not be a useful instrument of social control, providing an incentive for families to raise their children to the best of their abilities and to remonstrate with those who have gone astray, in hopes that some residual conscience may restrain them from tarnishing the good name of those who have been closest to them?

Family disgrace has proven to be a powerful instrument of social control in Japan, for example, though no one can doubt that individual injustices result from innocent family members' suffering from shame generated by the misdeeds of guilty relatives. The point here is not to be for or against such practices on a blanket basis. The more limited objective is to illustrate how radically differently we must proceed if our framework is one of cosmic justice rather than traditional justice.

The concept of merit adds insult to misfortune and arrogance to achievement. In an era when even lower-income members of Western societies seldom suffer hunger or physical deprivation, nevertheless the concept of merit provides them with grounds to fear and resent the disdain of others—whether that disdain is real or imagined. Where the widely varying fortunes of individuals and groups are seen as consequences of innumerable and ever-changing cross-currents, resulting differences in amenities should not provoke the same bitterness as in times and places where hunger, cold, and disease were the consequences of being less fortunate. Yet the concept of merit and the quest for cosmic justice can generate bitterness over differences that are far less consequential in themselves. It is one thing to be bitter because one cannot feed one's children and something very different to be resentful because one cannot afford designer jeans or expensive watches that keep no better time than cheap watches.

The Costs of Justice

With justice, as with equality, the question is not whether more is better, but whether it is better at all costs. We need to consider what those who believe in the vision of cosmic justice seldom want to consider—the nature of those costs and how they change the very nature of justice itself.

There are so many very different conceptions of justice that we need to begin with some examples of things that most of us can readily agree are unjust. Primogeniture—the practice of leaving an estate entirely to the eldest son—is something that most of us today would consider unjust to the other children. Arbitrarily selecting the ruler of a nation by a similar principle would likewise be widely objected to on moral grounds, among other objections to monarchy.

The purpose of primogeniture was of course to keep an estate intact from generation to generation. The point was not simply to make a given sum of wealth in one individual's hands larger than it would be if the land were shared. The point was to make the total wealth available *to the family as a whole* larger than it would have been under equal inheritance, where it would have been broken up into smaller and smaller pieces with the succeeding generations—creating economic inefficiencies that reduce the total value of the fragmented estate. Primogeniture relied on family ties and a sense of duty to guide the eldest son in looking out for his younger siblings.

Land was often worth more when it could be farmed in one piece than the sum total of smaller separate pieces after being subdivided. There are what economists call "economies of scale" in production and these can be lost as land is fragmented over time by being repeatedly divided equally among heirs. The poverty in a number of countries has been attributed to the fact that there are minute landholdings in those countries,[20] with a given farmer often having several of these tiny plots—inherited from different family branches—located at some distance from one another, requiring his working day to be similarly broken up and time lost in transit from one place to another. In short, cosmic justice for heirs can mean unnecessary poverty for society as a whole.

This by itself does not necessarily justify primogeniture. It simply says that the costs of achieving justice matter. Another way of saying the same thing is that *justice at all costs* is not justice. What, after all, is an injustice but the arbitrary imposition of a cost—whether economic, psychic, or other—on an innocent person? And if correcting this injustice imposes another arbitrary cost on another innocent person, is that not also an injustice? In the world of today, where most wealth is no longer in land but in financial assets which can be divided among heirs without such high costs, a very different situation exists, but this is not to say that primogeniture, when and where it existed in a different world, was without any rational or moral foundation.

Even those who proclaim the principles of justice, and call these principles more important than other benefits, as Professor

Rawls does, seem unlikely to act on such principles in real life, given the costs of doing so. Imagine that a ship is sinking in the ocean with 300 passengers on board and only 200 life-preservers. The only just solution is that everyone drown. But most of us would probably prefer the *unjust* solution, that 200 lives be saved, even if they are no more deserving than those who perish. We would probably prefer it even if we suspected that the most selfish and ruthless of those on board would probably end up with the life-preservers.

Even in less urgent circumstances, a similar principle applies. Imagine that Professor Rawls has arranged an important and remunerative lecture tour in Europe, only to discover on the eve of his departure date from America that (1) an unjust local tax assessment of $100 has been made against him, that (2) he has documents which can prove conclusively that he owes no such tax, and that (3) the time limits within which he is legally allowed to challenge the assessment are such that he would have to cancel his European lecture tour in order to achieve the just result to which he is entitled. Does anyone imagine that Professor Rawls would cancel his lecture tour, rather than pay the unjust tax? More to the point, if he did cancel the tour in order to fight that tax, would we regard him as a rational man of high principle or as a doctrinaire, a moral exhibitionist, or an egomaniac?

Adam Smith and John Rawls each said that justice was the prime virtue of a society, and yet they said it in such different senses that they meant nearly opposite things. To Smith, it was essential for the very existence and survival of any society that there be some predictable order, with some degree of moral principle, so that people could pursue their lives with their minds at peace, and not destroy each other and the whole social order with unremitting strife over the distribution of financial or other benefits. To Rawls, in any society that is advanced beyond a certain minimum of physical requirements, more justice was categorically more important than more of any other benefit— more important than additional material progress, artistic achievement, or personal or national safety. In short, for Smith a certain measure of justice was a prerequisite for social survival but, beyond that point, justice was simply one among many social and individual benefits to be weighed against one another. By contrast, Rawls' justice remained the over-riding benefit in any society that could be considered civilized.

Precisely because we are not used to deciding categorically whether it is better or worse to have justice, it is deceptively easy to glide into the Rawlsian position that more justice is always better. Indeed, what makes Rawls' conception of justice significant beyond the ranks of professional philosophers is that he systematically articulated a conception and a vision that already formed the underlying foundation of much legal theory and social policy.

While the great arena for the discussion of cosmic justice has been in social policy, the concept has been applied even in international relations, in matters involving grave decisions about war and peace. During the 1930s, when the shadow of an impending war hung over Europe, and weighty questions of military preparedness and military alliances had to be decided, there were still people in the Western democracies who regarded the Treaty of Versailles that ended the First World War as having been unjust to Germany—which then became for them a reason to be tolerant of Hitler's policies and actions, as the Nazi regime began a massive military buildup, in preparation for wars of aggression.

Looking back at events over which no one now had any control distracted attention from the urgent need to build offsetting military power to deter a future war that would dwarf in its horrors even the appalling carnage of the First World War. Never has preoccupation with cosmic justice had a higher price. Yet the power of the concept was demonstrated by the fact that, in the face of the gravest dangers, it prompted many to look back at the past, instead of ahead to a future which threatened the devastation of a continent, the slaughter of tens of millions of human beings, and the attempted extermination of entire races.

When it comes to social policy as well, some of those who consider themselves the most forward-looking are in fact most likely to look backward at a history that is beyond anyone's power to change. An historian writing about Czechoslovakia, for example, said that the policies of this newly created state after the First World War were "to correct social injustice" and to "put right the historic wrongs of the seventeenth century."[21] Presumably, no one from the seventeenth century was still alive at the end of the First World War. One of the many contrasts between traditional justice and cosmic justice is that traditional justice involves the rules under which flesh-and-blood human beings interact, while cosmic justice encompasses not only contemporary individuals and groups, but also group abstractions extending over generations, or even centuries.

A similar approach is found in the United States today, where issues of group "reparations" have been raised—reparations to blacks for slavery or to the indigenous American Indian population for the dispossession of their ancestors and the collateral damage that went with it. Here again, the issue encompasses what can be called inter-temporal group abstractions, rather than simply flesh-and-blood contemporaries. Seldom is the claim made that black Americans alive at this moment are worse off than if their ancestors had been left in Africa. Any attempt to make that case with statistics on income, life expectancy, or numerous other variables would collapse like a house of cards. Ultimately, of course, what matters are not such objective data but how the individuals involved feel and react. Here no one can say—or rather, those who choose to make ringing denunciations cannot be conclusively contradicted by objective evidence, since objective evidence is irrelevant to how they feel. However, it may be worth noting that the number of contemporary black Americans who have immigrated to Africa does not begin to approach the number of contemporary Africans who have immigrated to the United States.

Nevertheless, it remains painfully clear that those people who were torn from their homes in Africa in centuries past and forcibly brought across the Atlantic in chains suffered not only horribly, but unjustly. Were they and their captors still alive, the reparations and the retribution owed would be staggering. Time and death, however, cheat us of such opportunities for justice, however galling that may be. We can, of course, create new injustices among our flesh-and-blood contemporaries for the sake of symbolic expiation, so that the son or daughter of a black doctor or executive can get into an elite college ahead of the son or daughter of a white factory worker or farmer, but only believers in the vision of cosmic justice are likely to take moral solace from that. We can only make our choices among alternatives actually available, and rectifying the past is not one of those options.

The situation of the indigenous peoples of the Western Hemisphere is even more problematical. The question as to whether flesh-and-blood people of indigenous ancestry today would have been better off had the Europeans not invaded can scarcely be asked, much less answered, because most flesh-and-blood contemporary American Indians would not exist if the Europeans had not invaded, since they are of European as well as indigenous ancestry. Nature is remarkably uncooperative with our moral categories. There is no way to unscramble an egg.

Again, the sufferings of the native peoples of the Western Hemisphere during the era of European invasion were monumental, not only from the wars and depredations of the conquerors, but even more so from the European diseases which decimated the peoples of North and South America, with 50 percent mortality rates being common in some Indian societies and 90 percent mortality rates not unheard of. But time, unlike videotape, does not go backwards.

A case might be made that those indigenous peoples of the Western Hemisphere who *would* exist today if Europeans had not invaded would be better off than those descendants of the aboriginal population (with and without admixtures of the invading races) who actually exist. It is by no means obvious that even this is true but, in any event, that is clearly an issue about inter-temporal abstractions, not flesh-and-blood human beings.

Believers in the quest for cosmic justice do not give up easily. In politics, in law, and in intellectual circles, statistical disparities between the achievements, performances, or rewards of one group and those of the general population are often regarded as proof of either the present-day consequences of past injustices or as evidence that the injustices of the past are persisting into the present as discrimination against the groups in question.[22] Sometimes disparities between black and white Americans are attributed to historic racial injustices in the United States, growing out of peculiarities of American history. Yet similar—and even larger—disparities, whether in income or IQ, can be found among groups in other countries with entirely different histories, lacking the very factors that are assumed to underlie black-white differences in the United States.

We have seen how easy it is to go wrong by wide margins when dealing with history. It is equally easy to go wrong with contemporary statistics. If one goes through enough numbers, one will eventually come upon some statistics that seem to fit one's vision. These are what might be called "Aha!" statistics. Other statistics which suggest opposite conclusions bring no "Aha!" but are more likely to be glided over and forgotten.

A set of statistics that set off journalistic and political firestorms in 1993 showed that black applicants for mortgage loans were turned down at a higher rate than white applicants. *The Washington Post* declared that a "racially biased system of home lending exists,"[23] and numerous other publications, politicians, and activists joined the chorus of denunciation. However, the very same set of statistics showed that white applicants were turned down a higher percentage of the time than Asian Americans. Yet these statistics brought no "Aha!"—no claim that whites were being discriminated against in favor of Asian Americans—because this was not part of the prevailing vision. In short, numbers are accepted as evidence when they agree with preconceptions, but not when they don't.

Statistical comparisons implicitly assume that the groups being compared are indeed comparable on the relevant variables. Very often, however, they are not even close to being comparable. Closer scrutiny of the mortgage lending data, for example, shows that minority applicants for home loans had larger debt burdens, poorer credit histories, sought loans covering a higher percentage of the value of the properties in question, and were also more likely to seek to finance multiple-dwelling units rather than single-family homes, the former being considered the more risky investment.[24] Even so, 72 percent of the minority mortgage-loan applications were approved, compared to 89 percent of the white mortgage-loan applications. This 17 percentage point difference shrank to 6 percentage points when relevant variables were held constant. Moreover, all of the remaining statistical difference could be traced to different loan approval rates at one bank. Why did the government not take legal action against this one white racist bank? Because it was neither white nor racist. It was a black-owned bank.[25]

Incidentally, all of this occurred while a wave of bankruptcies was sweeping through American lending institutions. The idea that these institutions were passing up desperately needed profits from paying customers when institutional survival was at stake might seem at least questionable to anyone with a rudimentary knowledge of economics. However, a rudimentary knowledge of economics is not a requirement for a career in politics, journalism, or the judiciary. Certainly it is not a prerequisite for colorful expressions of moral indignation.[26]

It would be possible to go through any number of other statistical comparisons and show why they are not valid.[27] But the more fundamental problem is with the presupposition that social groups would be proportionally represented in various activities or institutions, or at various income levels, in the absence of bias and discrimination. On the contrary, it is difficult to find any such even representation in any country or in any period of history, except where a government policy mandates quotas or preferences to achieve an artificial statistical "balance."

Those who believe in cosmic justice sometimes argue that this simply shows how widespread discrimination is. But many groups who are in no position to discriminate against anyone are over-represented in high-paying occupations, prestigious academic institutions, and numerous other desirable sectors of the economy and society. It would be possible to go through a long list of statistical disparities involving either people or things, where not even a plausible case for discrimination can be made. Here are just a few:

1. More than four-fifths of the doughnut shops in California are owned by people of Cambodian ancestry.[28]
2. In the early twentieth century, four-fifths of the world's sugar-processing machinery was made in Scotland.[29]
3. As of 1909, Italians in Buenos Aires owned more than twice as many food and drinking establishments as the native Argentines, more than three times as many shoe stores, and more than ten times as many barbershops.[30]
4. During the decade of the 1960s, the Chinese minority in Malaysia supplied between 80 and 90 percent of all university students in medicine, science, and engineering.[31]
5. In the early twentieth century, all of the firms in all of the industries producing the following products in

Brazil's state of Rio Grande do Sul were owned by people of German ancestry: trunks, stoves, paper, hats, neckties, leather, soap, glass, watches, beer, confections, and carriages.[32]

6. In eighteenth-century Russia, 209 out of 240 cloth factories in the province of Astrakhan were owned by Armenians.[33]

7. Of the 16,000 workers who built the East Africa Railway line from the port of Mombasa to Lake Victoria, 15,000 were from India.[34]

8. As of 1937, 91 percent of all greengrocers' licenses in Vancouver, Canada, were held by people of Japanese ancestry.[35]

9. Although less than 5 percent of Indonesia's population, ethnic Chinese have at one time run three-quarters of its 200 largest businesses.[36]

10. In the early 1920s, Jews were only 6 percent and 11 percent of the populations of Hungary and Poland, respectively, but they were more than half of all the doctors in both countries.[37]

This list could be extended many times over.[38]

Why are different groups so disproportionately represented in so many times and places? Perhaps the simplest answer is that there was no reason to have expected them to be statistically similar in the first place. Geographical, historical, demographic, cultural, and other variables make the vision of an even or random distribution of groups one without foundation.

Statistical disparities are of course not limited to racial groups or to male-female differences. Moreover, believers in the quest for cosmic justice often confuse the fate of statistical abstractions with the fate of flesh-and-blood human beings. Much has been written, for example, about how small percentages of the population receive large percentages of the nation's income or hold some large percentage of the nation's wealth. The implicit assumption is that we are talking about classes of people when, in the United States at least, we are in fact often talking about individuals at different stages of their lives.

The vast majority of the wealth of Americans is concentrated in the hands of people over fifty years of age. The average wealth in older families in the United States is some multiple of the average wealth in younger families. But these are not differences in social classes. Everyone who is old was once young and all the young are going to be old, except for those who die prematurely. Yet the *vision* of social classes remains impervious to these plain facts, and statistical abstractions are automatically seen as classes of people.

Studies which have followed individual Americans over a period of years have found that most do not stay in the same quintile of the income distribution for as long as a decade. The first of these studies was conducted by a group of academics of left-wing persuasion, who seemed to be thrown into disarray by their own findings, which were based on following the same individuals for eight years.[39] But none of this should be surprising. People are eight years older at the end of eight years. They have eight years more experience, eight years more seniority. If they have set up a business, they have had eight years in which to become better known and to attract more customers. In the professions, they have had eight years in which to build up a clientele. Why would they not be in higher income brackets at the end of eight years?

"The poor," who are often defined as the bottom 20 percent of the income distribution, are as transient in that role as the rich. Only 3 percent of the American population remained in the bottom 20 percent for as long as eight years. More who began in the bottom 20 percent had reached the top 20 percent by the end of that period than remained where they were. Yet "the poor" continue to be identified as the bottom 20 percent, instead of the 3 percent who remain at the bottom. Our intellectual discourse and our public policy are based on the statistical abstraction of 20 percent, rather than the flesh-and-blood 3 percent who are genuinely poor.

It is reminiscent of a story about someone who was told that, in New York City, someone is hit by a car every 20 minutes. "He must get awfully tired of that" was the response. But some of our most renowned intellectuals, not to mention moral and political leaders, commit the same mistake of thinking that it is the same people all the time when they talk about statistical abstractions as if they were talking about flesh-and-blood people who are rich and poor. The genuinely rich and the genuinely poor, put together, do not add up to even 10 percent of the American population.[40] Yet these two marginal groups are the central characters in the moral melodramas which dominate American politics, journalism, and even academic and judicial discourse.

CONSEQUENCES OF THE QUEST FOR COSMIC JUSTICE

Whatever the intellectual deficiencies of the vision of cosmic justice, it has become politically entrenched in many countries around the world. Its consequences are therefore important for that reason alone. What are those consequences?

Those pursuing the quest for cosmic justice have tended to assume that the consequences would be what they intended—which is to say, that the people subject to government policies would be like pieces on a chessboard, who could be moved here and there to carry out a grand design, without concern for their own responses. But both the intended beneficiaries and those on whom the costs of those benefits would fall have often reacted in ways unexpected by those who have sought cosmic justice.

Those given legal entitlements to various compensatory benefits have, for example, developed a sense of entitlement. As a group leader in India asked: "Are we not entitled to jobs just because we are not as qualified?"[41] A Nigerian likewise spoke of "the tyranny of skills."[42] Black American college students planning to go on to post-graduate education were found by one study to feel no sense of urgency about needing to prepare themselves academically "because they believe that certain rules would simply be set aside for them."[43]

A similar lack of urgency was found by a study of Malaysian students in Malaysia, where they are legally entitled to preferential access to coveted positions in government and in the private economy.[44] In the American Virgin Islands, even school children have excused their own lack of academic and behavioral standards by pointing out that government jobs will be waiting for them when they grow up—jobs for which their West Indian classmates will not be eligible, even though the latter perform better academically and behave themselves better in school as well, because the West Indians are not American citizens.[45]

There has been a particularly tragic consequence of the quest for cosmic justice for young black Americans. Just as some parents make the mistake of talking around small children as if they cannot hear or understand, so those promoting a vision of cosmic injustices as the cause of all the problems of black Americans have failed to understand the consequences of this vision for young blacks who do not yet have either the personal experience or the maturity to weigh those words against reality. The net result in many ghetto schools has been the development of an attitude of hostility to learning or to conforming to ordinary standards of behavior in society. Worse, those young black students who do wish to get an education, to speak correct English, and to behave in ways compatible with getting along with others, are accused of "acting white"—betraying the race—and are subject to both social pressures and outright intimidation and violence.

It would be hard to imagine a more devastating self-destruction of a whole generation's future. Many of the politicians, intellectuals, and others who have loudly and often proclaimed that discrimination explains all, or virtually all, black-white differences are themselves appalled and baffled by this turn of events. Yet these attitudes among young blacks make perfect sense if the vision that is presented to them is true. Why study and discipline yourself in preparation for the adult world if the deck is completely stacked against you anyway? At least you can show that you are not a sucker who is taken in. What these students are doing is consistent with the vision that is presented to them, however tragically counterproductive it may be in the world of reality.

This pattern of able and ambitious young people being held back by fear of the envy and resentment of their peers is not limited to blacks or to the United States. Similar patterns have been found among working-class youngsters in the east end of London—a pattern aptly characterized by an observer there as "loathsomely insidious."[46]

What of those whose interests are to be sacrificed in the quest for cosmic justice? They too respond quite rationally, in light of the options presented to them. Individuals may cease to strive as hard for posts that they are less likely to get or may remove themselves from the whole society, as some highly educated Chinese have done in Malaysia and some highly educated Indians have done in Fiji, or as highly skilled and highly entrepreneurial Huguenots removed themselves from France in centuries past.

In the United States, where an employer's failure to have a workforce ethnically representative of the local population is taken as evidence of discrimination, employers can choose locations where they are not near concentrations of blacks and thus minimize their legal risks. Of course, this means that blacks end up losing job opportunities as a result of being preferentially entitled to jobs. Whether the jobs lost this way are greater or less than the jobs gained where local employers accede to government policy is an empirical question. However, this question attracts remarkably little attention or interest from those zealous for symbolic "social justice." It may also be worth noting that the rate of progress of blacks, and especially of low-income blacks, during the era of affirmative action policies has been less than that under the "equal opportunity" policies which preceded it, or even before equal opportunity policies.[47]

In this and other circumstances, the quest for cosmic justice does not necessarily mean an end result of greater equality or justice than under policies meant to carry out traditional, mundane human justice. The only clear-cut winners in the quest for cosmic justice are those who believe in the vision it projects — a vision in which those believers are so morally and/or intellectually superior to others that their own relentless pursuit of this vision is seen as all that offers some modicum of hope to those who would otherwise be victims of the lesser people who make up the rest of society. It is a very self-flattering vision — and hence one not easily given up. Evidence to the contrary is not only likely to be dismissed, but is often blamed on the malevolence or dishonesty of those who present such evidence.

It is difficult to explain the fury and ruthlessness of those with this vision of cosmic justice, whenever they are challenged, by the simple fact that they consider policy A to be better than policy B. What is at stake for them is not merely a policy option, but a whole vision of the world and of their own place in that world. No wonder it is seldom possible to have rational discussions of some of these issues.

Nobody should be happy with cosmic injustices. The real questions are:

1. What can we do about them — and at what cost?
2. What should we do collectively about them — and how much should we leave up to individuals themselves?

Just as those seeking cosmic justice must become aware of the enormous costs of their quest, so those who see cosmic justice as a dangerous mirage must also recognize how naturally people of all philosophical persuasions prefer the vision embodied in this quest and attempt to practice it, whenever circumstances permit without ruinous costs or dangerous risks. Not only have such conservative intellectual leaders as Milton Friedman and

Friedrich Hayek acknowledged and lamented the undeserved misfortunes of some and the huge windfall gains of others, the behavior of many highly traditional people reveals similar concerns, expressed for example in massive philanthropy, but also in everyday life. Even the most conservative families often operate on the Marxian principle, "From each according to his abilities, to each according to his needs," when they spend heavily for the present and future benefit of children who are themselves earning no money. Indeed, this pattern sometimes extends into the children's adulthood and it often extends to other family members struck by medical or financial disasters.

The very attractiveness of cosmic justice in the close personal relations and mutually felt *reciprocal* obligations within a family makes it a seductive danger as a government policy of "entitlements" (implying *no* reciprocal obligations) in a large, impersonal society. The alternative to political crusades and government programs is not that we should "do nothing," as it is sometimes thoughtlessly phrased. There has never been a moment in the entire history of the United States when nothing was being done to offset the undeserved misfortunes of the poor and the disadvantaged. Indeed, as Milton Friedman has pointed out, the period of the greatest opposition to the role of government in the economy in the nineteenth century was also a period of an unprecedented growth of private philanthropy. It was also a period of private social uplift efforts by volunteers all across America. Such efforts, incidentally, had a dramatic effect in reducing crime and other social ills such as alcoholism, so these were hardly ineffectual gestures. Indeed, they were far more effective than the more massive government-run programs that began in the 1960s.

Organized philanthropy and individual efforts to help those born into less fortunate circumstances have been as widespread among those who have opposed political "solutions" as among those who have promoted them, even if the former have not paraded their compassion as much as the latter. Only when Adam Smith's personal records were opened after his death was it discovered how much of his modest wealth had been given away to help others. Milton Friedman has set up a foundation to promote school vouchers, in order to try to rescue children whose parents are too poor to enable them to escape the inferior education they receive in public schools. Numerous other conservative individuals have done similar things, including those whose fortunes went into the Carnegie, Ford, and Rockefeller foundations, where others later changed the focus to promotion of a very different vision from those of the donors. Such plain facts may be surprising to some only because they do not fit the prevailing vision, however widely or however long they have fit the facts.

The question is not whether undeserved misfortunes shall be addressed. The question is whether they will be addressed politically, rather than in the numerous other ways in which they have been, are being, and will be addressed, usually without the high costs, counterproductive results, and dangers to the whole fabric of society that the politicizing of such misfortunes has produced repeatedly in countries around the world. At a minimum, it is necessary to understand the distinction between establishing prospective rules for the behavior of flesh-and-blood human beings toward one another and trying ad hoc to retrospectively adjust the cosmos to our tastes.

Not only does cosmic justice differ from traditional justice, and conflict with it, more momentously cosmic justice is irreconcilable with personal freedom based on the rule of law. Traditional justice can be mass-produced by impersonal prospective rules governing the interactions of flesh-and-blood human beings, but cosmic justice must be hand-made by holders of power who impose their own decisions on how these flesh-and-blood individuals should be categorized into abstractions and how these abstractions should then be forcibly configured to fit the vision of the power-holders. Merely the power to select beneficiaries is an enormous power, for it is also the power to select victims—and to reduce both to the role of supplicants of those who hold this power.

One of the crucial differences between political and non-political ways of dealing with undeserved misfortunes is that the non-political approaches do not acquire the fatal rigidities of law nor require either the vision or the reality of helplessness and dependency. Nor does it require the demonization of those who think otherwise or the polarization of society. Moreover, the amount of help and the circumstances of help can be tailored to the individual circumstances of the recipients in a way that is not possible when the rigidities of law create "rights" to what others have earned, independent of one's own behavior or the role of that behavior in the misfortunes being suffered.

Most important of all, attempts at bettering the lot of society in general, as well as the unfortunate in particular, need not take the form of direct aid at all. Rather, these efforts can more effectively take the form of creating economic and other circumstances in which individuals can themselves find "life, liberty and the pursuit of happiness." Such an approach does not seek to feed the hungry but to establish conditions in which no one has to be hungry in the first place, circumstances in which there are jobs available for those willing to work. Its emphasis is not on helping those in poverty but on getting them out of poverty and preventing others from falling into poverty.

Economic development has been the most successful of all anti-poverty policies. It was not very long ago, as history is measured, when such things as oranges or cocoa were the luxuries of the rich and when it was considered an extravagance for the President of the United States to have a bathtub with running water installed in the White House. Within the twentieth century, such things as automobiles, telephones, and refrigerators went from being luxuries of the rich to being common among the general population, all within the span of one generation.

Material well-being is of course not everything. Justice matters as well. But, whatever one's vision of a just world, what is crucial is to recognize that (1) different visions lead to radically different practical policies, that (2) we shall continue to talk past one another so long as we do not recognize that cosmic justice changes the very meaning of the plainest words, and that (3) whatever we choose to do, it should be based on a clear understanding of the costs and dangers of the actual alternatives, not simply the heady feeling of exaltation produced by particular words or visions. Recognizing that many people "through no fault of their own" have windfall losses, while those same people—and others—also have windfall gains, the time is long overdue to recognize also that taxpayers *through no fault of their own* have been forced to subsidize the moral adventures which exalt self-anointed social philosophers. Victims of violent crimes have been forced to bear even more painful losses from those same moral adventures.

47

There is no question that a world in which cosmic justice prevailed would be a better world than a world limited to traditional justice. However, it is one thing to rail against the fates, but no one should confuse that with a serious critique of existing society, much less a basis for constructing a better one.

There is an ancient fable about a dog with a bone in his mouth. He looked down into a pool of water and saw a reflection that looked to him like another dog with another bone— and that other bone seemed to be larger than his bone. Determined to get the other bone instead, the dog opened his mouth and prepared to jump into the water. This of course caused his own bone to drop into the water and be lost. Cosmic justice is much like that illusory bone and it too can cause us to lose what is attainable in quest of the unattainable.

II

~

The Mirage of Equality

Many a man has cherished for years as his hobby
some vague shadow of an idea, too meaningless
to be positively false . . .

—CHARLES SANDERS PEIRCE

Equality, like justice, is one of the most fateful—and unde-fined—words of our times. Whole societies can be, and have been, jeopardized by the passionate pursuit of this elusive notion. There is nothing wrong with equality in itself. In fact, there is much that is attractive about the idea. At the very least, glaring inequalities are unattractive, even for those who accept them as either inevitable, like death, or as the lesser of alterna-tive evils. But to equate the attractiveness of the concept with a mandate for public policy aimed at equality is to assume that politicizing inequality is free of costs and dangers, when in fact such politicization can have very high costs and very grave dan-gers. The abstract desirability of equality, like the abstract desir-ability of immortality, is beside the point when choosing what practical course of action to follow. What matters is what we are prepared to do, to risk, or to sacrifice, in pursuit of what can turn out to be a mirage.

Processes designed to create greater equality cannot be judged by that goal but must be examined in terms of the processes created in pursuit of that goal. It is the nature of these processes—including their addictiveness and the never-ending strife they can engender if equality proves to be impossible to achieve—which creates the dangers. In short, the problem is with the mirage, not with the realization of an idea that seems unlikely ever to be realized.

MEANINGS OF EQUALITY

One of the reasons why equality may be impossible to achieve is that merely defining it opens up a bottomless pit of complications.

Numbers may be equal $(2 + 3 = 5)$ because they have only one dimension, magnitude. But equality among multidimensional entities, even inanimate and abstract entities like the Gross National Product, may be impossible to define—much less achieve—when one nation's GNP includes much more of products A, B, and C, while another nation's GNP includes much more of products X, Y, and Z. Only by finding some common denominator that can be applied to these disparate assortments is it possible to say which country has the higher total GNP—and even then, this common denominator may be so arbitrary that it cannot command the acquiescence of those whose definition is different, and who therefore cannot regard equality as defined by this arbitrary standard as being anything other than inequality by the standard they prefer.

In the case of determining which country has a higher Gross National Product, the first country may have a higher GNP if the common denominator is the price of goods as measured by using official exchange rates, while the second country may have a higher GNP if the test is which country could actually purchase all of the other country's GNP in the international marketplace and still have something left over. By the first criterion, Japan has a higher per capita output than the United States but, by the second criterion, the United States has a 25 percent higher per capita output than Japan.[1]

Since human beings are even more multidimensional, defining equality among them becomes even more problematical and ultimately arbitrary, quite aside from the subsequent difficulties of achieving whatever equality might be defined.

Economic equality, for example, may be achievable only by political measures which require vast concentrations of power in a relatively few hands in government—and even this momentous exchange of economic inequality for political inequality may leave untouched the vast spectrum of other inequalities in intelligence, talent, physical appearance, charm, articulation, etc., which may have more influence on many individuals' prospects of happiness than the economic inequalities that have been addressed at such high cost. However, since economic inequalities are a central focus of those seeking a more egalitarian society, it may be useful to explore some of the difficulties in merely defining and determining how much economic inequality exists already, quite aside from the costs and dangers in trying to change the economic system in some fundamental way, in hopes of more egalitarian results.

Economic Equality and Inequality

Ironically, economic inequalities, which are widely regarded as far more serious than inequalities in sports, for example, are far less well documented or even well defined. It has long been a common practice in sports statistics to follow the same individual over a period of years, but this is a relatively new departure in statistics on income inequalities. Even now, most of the statistics that are thrown around concerning "the rich" and "the poor" are aggregate statistics about income strata *as of a given moment,* even though most Americans do not stay in the same quintile of the income distribution for as long as a decade. Given this transience of membership in the various income brackets, it is possible to understand some otherwise puzzling statistics on the lifestyles of "the poor."

People in the bottom quintile of the income distribution spend nearly two dollars for every dollar of income they receive.[2] Two-thirds of the statistically defined "poor" have air-conditioning, and more than half own a car or truck. More than one-fourth of "the poor" own two cars and/or trucks and hundreds of thousands of them own homes costing more than $150,000.[3] Puzzling as such anomalies might seem if we were discussing an enduring class of genuinely poor people, they are understandable in a statistical category which includes many transients. In any given year, many entrepreneurs may be earning not only low incomes but *negative* incomes as their businesses incur losses. Professionals, entertainers, and others may also suffer off years that leave them in the bottom 20 percent for that year. Many members of high school and college graduating classes enter the labor force in the middle of the year, earning only about half of what they will normally be earning when they work the entire year. Unless they find very high-paying jobs, their half-year earnings may well leave them statistically among "the poor."

Middle-class or wealthy people are unlikely to divest themselves of all the accoutrements of their lifestyle just because they are having an off year, especially when they have financial resources and/or credit that will see them through till their situation improves again. In short, many of those in the bottom 20 percent of the income distribution are not "poor" in any meaningful sense and do not live like people who expect to remain there. Since only 3 percent of the American population remains in the bottom quintile for as long as eight years, it is hardly surprising that so many of those who are defined as being in poverty as of any given year do not act as if they are.

In contrast to the carefulness with which sports statistics are kept, most statistics about "the poor" totally ignore their financial assets. Thus someone with a million dollars in the bank, or who owns property worth several million, will be counted among "the poor" during off years in his business or profession, when his revenues for a particular year barely exceed his costs for that particular year, or when his net income for that year may be negative. Politically or ideologically, of course, incentives are to maximize the number of people who can be counted as "poor," in justification of movements or policies ostensibly aimed at reducing poverty.

The radically different picture produced by following actual flesh-and-blood human beings over time, as distinguished from looking at statistics for a given moment in time, applies not only to "the poor" but also to "the rich." The typical Hollywood movie version of the rich—someone born in a mansion, heir to a fortune, educated in snooty private schools and Ivy League colleges—bears little resemblance to actual millionaires studied in the 1990s—or in the 1890s, for that matter. A 1996 study found that four-fifths of all the American millionaires studied earned their fortunes within their own lifetimes. So did an 1892 study.[4]

The social origins of a group of individuals with net worths of $10 million each or more was inadvertently revealed at a gathering sponsored by a financial organization, where exquisite food and drink had been prepared for a group more like the Hollywood millionaire or "the rich" of political rhetoric:

> To make sure our decamillionaire respondents felt comfortable during the interview, we rented a posh penthouse on Manhattan's fashionable East Side. We also hired two gourmet food designers. They put together a menu of four pâtés and three kinds of caviar. To accompany this, the designers suggested a case of high-quality 1970 Bordeaux plus a case of a "wonderful" 1973 cabernet sauvignon. . . . During the subsequent two-hour interview, the nine decamillionaire respondents shifted constantly in their chairs. Occasionally they glanced at the buffet. But not one touched the pâté or drank our vintage wines. We knew they were hungry, but all they ate were the gourmet crackers.[5]

These multimillionaires were clearly in an unfamiliar setting, based on a lifestyle very different from the way they actually lived. Unlike Hollywood movie millionaires, most American millionaires do not have a lavish lifestyle. The average cost of their automobiles — $24,800 — is only a few thousand dollars more than that of the average American's automobile and is well below the cost of such luxury cars as the Cadillac or Lexus.[6] Twice as many American millionaires have a Sears credit card as have a credit card from Neiman Marcus.[7] Most have never paid as much as $400 for a suit. For every millionaire who buys a $1,000 suit, six or more non-millionaires buy one.[8]

In short, neither the rich nor the poor match the classic picture of a class into which people are born, live, and die — and in which they maintain a lifestyle born of that permanence. The persistently rich and persistently poor, put together, are not a major segment of the American population, though political issues are often framed as if they were. As already noted, only 3 percent of Americans remain in the bottom 20 percent for as long as eight years. Only 3.5 percent of the American population have a net worth of one million dollars or more,[9] even though net worth literally includes the kitchen sink, as well as other household assets, clothing, pension fund equity, and other assets that could not be turned into ready cash. Nevertheless, even with this generous definition, both the rich and the poor—put together—add up to less than 7 percent of the American population. Nevertheless, great political and ideological battles are often fought as if these were the central groups in the society, rather than the other 93 percent who are in no meaningful sense either rich or poor.

A major factor in both income and wealth is age. Those who have worked for many years tend to have advanced in their careers to higher-paying positions and to have accumulated more assets, whether in the form of money in the bank or a pension fund, or equity in their homes. People in their sixties have persistently had higher incomes than people in their twenties and much higher net worths. In short, membership in various income brackets tends to be transient, in the American economy at least, due both to age and to the ordinary ups and downs of individuals' careers and of the surrounding economy. Yet that fact has had very little effect on visions, crusades, or the rhetoric attacking "inequality."

Equality and Inequality of Performance
Thus far, in speaking of equality among human beings, we have mentioned only equality of benefits. But most benefits must be

produced and another dimension of equality is equality of productivity or performance. Egalitarians are offended if any race, gender, or other social groupings are said to be inferior in productivity or performance, especially if it is claimed that they are innately so. But merely defining performance uniquely can be virtually impossible, even in a narrow field.

To deliberately choose an example with no ideological overtones to confuse the issue, Ty Cobb's lifetime batting average was 25 points higher than Babe Ruth's, but Ruth hit far more home runs. To arrive at some common denominator in which to compare their batting performances, you must make some ultimately arbitrary determination as to how many singles are the equivalent of how many home runs—and all this quite aside from differences between Cobb and Ruth as outfielders or base runners, or the fact that Ruth was one of the top pitchers in baseball during his early career. Note again that all these complications arise merely in defining equality of performance in one aspect of a narrow specialty like professional baseball. We have not even begun to address the question as to how other ballplayers might be made equal in performance to either Cobb or Ruth, much less what equality of performance would mean when comparing performances across a vast spectrum of fields of endeavor.

One of the things that makes sports fascinating to so many people are the endless debates as to who was "the greatest" in a particular sport, or even in a particular specialty within a given sport—the greatest quarterback, shortstop, welterweight, center, goalie, etc. These debates are never resolved, precisely because there is no common denominator, even when the facts are extensively documented, beyond dispute, and widely available.

The Baseball Encyclopedia, for example, contains nearly three thousand pages of detailed statistics, printed in small type and covering every player in the history of major league baseball. Yet the debates rage on, because defining equality—and its corollaries, superiority and inferiority—is ultimately a conceptual, rather than an empirical, dilemma.

To question equality, whether in concept or in policy application, is not to advocate inequality. The conceptual difficulties in defining who is equal apply as well to defining who is superior and who is inferior. These difficulties are not insurmountable, but they do require some further specifications, and these specifications must ultimately be arbitrary. Some of these difficulties are apparent when we turn to concrete examples involving equality or inequalities of income and wealth, equality or inequalities of performance, equality or inequalities of merit, all at the individual level. Difficulties also arise when considering group equality or inequalities as regards either minority groups within a given society or cultural equality or inequality as regards one society or civilization compared to another.

Culture versus Equality
At all stages of history, vast disparities in performance have been commonplace among peoples, nations, regions, and many other groupings of human beings. These disparities have been economic, military, technological, and so on, across a vast spectrum of human differences. Races have been just one of the many groupings which have differed in performance, but these differences have been equally profound among other groupings which have no genetic basis. Moreover, races which have clearly been far more technologically or organizationally advanced than

others at one stage of history have been equally far behind those other races in another.

China, for example, was far more advanced than any nation in Europe, in many technological and organizational ways, for many centuries. Yet, for the past several centuries, the roles of China and Europe have been reversed. Even within Europe, for most of the recorded history of the continent, Southern Europeans have been more advanced than those of the north. Greece had Plato and Aristotle, the Acropolis, and the Colossus at Rhodes, at a time when much of northern Europe consisted of illiterate tribal societies living primitive lives. Yet the technological, economic, and scientific frontier of Europe has for the past few centuries been its northern and western nations.

Clearly the question as to whether there have been large performance differences between peoples, as of a given time, is quite different from the question as to whether those differences are racial or genetic in origin. Even so, resistance to acknowledging superior performances has in recent times been fierce, determined, and ingenious, even if not always ingenuous.

The most sweeping denials of performance superiority have been based on redefining them out of existence as culturally biased "perceptions" and "stereotypes." Those who take this approach of cultural relativism acknowledge only differences but no superiority. Yet all cultures serve practical purposes, as well as being symbolic and emotional, and they serve these practical purposes more efficiently or less efficiently—not just in the opinions of particular observers but, more importantly, in the *practices* of the societies themselves, which borrow from other cultures and discard their own ways of doing particular things.

Western civilization, for example, has abandoned Roman numerals for mathematical work, in favor of a very different numbering system originating in India and conveyed to the West by Arabs. The West has also abandoned scrolls in favor of paper, and scribes in favor of printing, in each case choosing things originating in China over things indigenous to Western culture. All over the world, peoples have abandoned their own bows and arrows for guns, wherever they have had a choice. Much of the story of the advancement of the human race has been a story of massive cultural borrowings, which have created a modern world technology, as much at home in Japan as in Europe or the United States.

Whatever the theories of cultural relativists, the actual practices of human beings in virtually all cultures throughout history contradict the notion that it is just a matter of "perceptions." These practices of human beings across the planet and down through history—the preferences revealed by cultural borrowing—provide a common denominator in which particular products of many cultures can be compared. In this common scheme of valuation, it is clear that some economies, for example, perform much better than others. Nor is this merely a culture-bound perception. Many Japanese products find numerous buyers in societies culturally very different from that of Japan.

Within societies, as between societies, equality of performance is not to be found. As the distinguished French historian Fernand Braudel put it: "In no society have all regions and all parts of the population developed equally."[10] Performance equality is the most difficult of all kinds of equality to believe in, on any basis other than sheer dogma. The same man is not even equal to himself on different days, much less at different periods

of life. However, denials and evasions of performance differences take many forms. A vast literature and powerful legal and
political doctrines in many countries proclaim intergroup disparities in representation or rewards to be "inequities" due either
to overt discrimination or to subconscious bias by individuals,
institutions, or "society."

Virtually no one has seriously denied that discrimination and
bias have resulted in various inequalities. It is the converse
proposition—that discrimination or bias can be inferred from
statistical inequalities—which is the reigning *non sequitur* of our
times, both intellectually and politically. To prove statistically
that the observed patterns of representation or reward are not
due to random chance is considered to be virtual proof that
they are due to discrimination—not to performance differences.
The implicit assumption is that a more or less even or random
representation or reward for performance could be expected, in
the absence of institutional or societal policies and practices
which disadvantage one group compared to others. Yet there has
never been an even or random world, even in matters not controlled by the biases of others. Not only performance differences
but also differences in luck and in many other factors wholly dis-
rupt the simple picture of an even, regular, or balanced world.

In the case of many social disparities, the beneficiaries have
often been powerless minorities with no way to discriminate
against the majority populations of their respective countries.
The history of the Jews in Eastern Europe, the "overseas
Chinese" in Southeast Asia, the Lebanese in West Africa, and
emigrants from India in Fiji are just some of the examples.
Innumerable factors are behind these disparities, including not
only performance differences but also differences in median

age (often differing by a decade or more from one racial or ethnic group to another), differences in regional distribution, and other differences that may be obvious, speculative, or unknown. What is wholly unsubstantiated is the prevailing assumption that the world would be random or even, in the absence of discrimination or bias by individuals, institutions, or "society."

The factors operating against performance equality are far too numerous, beginning with the physical settings in which different peoples have evolved culturally and economically. Geography is not egalitarian. The very ground that people stand on differs radically in fertility, topography, mineral wealth, and other characteristics. Navigable waterways are abundant in Western Europe and painfully scarce in sub-Saharan Africa. Large beasts of burden, such as horses and oxen, which for centuries played vital roles in the economic life of many parts of the world, were totally lacking in the entire Western Hemisphere before Columbus arrived. It is not uncommon for rainfall on one side of a mountain range to be ten times what it is on the other side, making for radically different agricultural prospects for the people in the two regions. Geography is brutally oblivious to human desires for equality.

It is not simply that economic levels vary widely for different regions of the earth, as a result of fortuitous geographical differences. More fundamentally, *the people themselves* vary in their cultural development, according to whether their respective geographical settings facilitate or impede their economic development and their exposure to a wider world of economic and cultural interactions.

How could Eskimos have acquired the skills and experience needed to grow pineapples or other tropical crops? How could the peoples of the Himalayas have learned to navigate on the high seas? How would Scandinavians or Polynesians know as much about camels as the Beduins of the Sahara—or the Beduins know as much about fishing as the Scandinavians or Polynesians? Given that the mineral deposits that were central to the industrial revolution neither existed in the Balkans nor could have been transported there without prohibitive costs, how could emigrants from the Balkans have brought with them to North America or to Australia the industrial skills possessed by people from the mineral-rich industrial heartlands of Germany or Britain?

People living on isolated islands in the sea, in remote mountain communities, or in other geographical settings that limit their cultural exposures, tend generally to lag behind the technological, organizational, and other developments among people more favorably situated. When the Spaniards invaded the Canary Islands in the fifteenth century, they found people of a Caucasian race living at a stone age level. So were the Australian aborigines when the British encountered them.

Around the world, according to Braudel, mountains "remain almost always on the fringe of the great waves of civilization" for civilizations "are an urban and lowland achievement."[11] Cities have long been in the vanguard of human advancement all around the world and over centuries of history. But cities do not arise equally in all geographic settings. In the millennia before the railroad appeared, most cities arose on navigable waterways. Such waterways are vastly more common in Western Europe than in sub-Saharan Africa and so are cities.

Differences in location mean that the sun beats down on different parts of the world with different intensity, making for profound differences in climate and, therefore, in agriculture and diseases. The availability of water for drinking, farming, or transportation likewise differs radically across the planet—and, even when two regions are both served by rivers, the contrast between those rivers can affect the economic viability of the regions they serve and the cultural development of the peoples within those regions. While rivers in Western Europe may be flowing year-around, rivers in Russia may be frozen for months at a time and rivers in Africa may be navigable for only limited stretches, due to cascades and waterfalls, not to mention drastic seasonal changes in rainfall.

It would be miraculous if all these—and many other—geographical variables worked out in such a way that each group's evolution in its particular physical setting produced the same levels of skills in the same fields of endeavor as that of other peoples elsewhere, even during a given era, much less over the centuries and millennia of human history.

Such geographically influenced disparities as of a given time often persist over time, even when peoples move from one geographical setting to another, taking with them a particular set of skills and a whole mental universe, transplanting it into a different setting, where they compete with indigenous people and with others transplanted from other settings that produced different skills and different cultures. Scottish highlanders long differed culturally from Scottish lowlanders, not only in Scotland itself but also in the United States and Australia, where the lowlanders were far more economically successful, as they were in Scotland.[12] Similar disparities have marked the respective histories of German Jews versus Eastern European Jews or of Gujaratis versus Tamils from India, among others.

Even putting aside all the differences growing out of geographical origins and their cultural consequences, demographic differences alone operate powerfully against equality of performance. No one expects small children to perform as well as adults with decades of education and experience—and groups differ significantly in the respective proportions of their populations which consist of children and which consist of those who are middle-aged adults. Moreover, such intergroup differences in demographic characteristics are common in societies around the world.

In the United States, for example, the median age of Jews is decades older than the median age of Puerto Ricans. Even if Puerto Ricans and Jews were identical in every other respect, they would still not be equally represented, in proportion to their respective populations, in jobs requiring long years of experience, or in homes for the elderly, or in activities associated with youth, such as sports or crime. The point here is not to claim that age alone explains most income or wealth differences. The point is that age differences alone are enough to preclude the equality that is presumed to exist in the absence of discrimination. Many other factors also make that vision an impossible one.

Despite the ease with which some discussions of income glide from the statistical category of inequality to the moral category of inequity, there is nothing requiring either special explanation or special justification in the fact that a young man beginning his career in his twenties is unlikely to be earning as much as his father in his forties, who has decades more experience, as well as more time in which to build a reputation. Since the father is also likely to have heavier financial responsibilities—for sending children through college or preparing for his own retirement and the growing medical expenses associated with age—statistical differences in income do not necessarily reflect corresponding differences in economic well-being. The son may even be able to afford some amenities or luxuries which his father cannot afford on a higher income.

Within given families, there are performance differences on mental tests as between the first-born child and later children. A study of National Merit Scholarship finalists separated out the first-born from the later siblings and discovered that more than half of these finalists were first-borns—even in five-child families.[13] A later study showed that IQ differences among siblings translated into income differences between them of a magnitude comparable to those between unrelated individuals with different IQs.[14] If you cannot achieve equality of performance among people born to the same parents and raised under the same roof, how realistic is it to expect to achieve it across broader and deeper social divisions?

The mere fact that families differ in size adds to statistical inequalities. Statistics on how the income of the top fifth of families compares with the income of the bottom fifth are misleading when they do not take into account that the top fifth of families contains more *people* than the bottom fifth. Families and households have differed in size from one era to another, from one group to another, and from one income bracket to another. For example, there are more than 50 percent more people per household earning $75,000 and up as per household earning under $15,000. That is one of the reasons for their differences in income: People earn money and more people tend to earn more money.

There are more than twice as many income-earners per household in households earning $75,000 and up as per household earning under $15,000. The top 20 percent of income-earning families supply 29 percent of all workers who work 50 weeks or more per year, while the bottom 20 percent supply just 7 percent of such workers. There are very mundane explanations for many of the statistical differences that some seek to explain in more sinister and melodramatic terms.

Some people have claimed that groups also differ genetically in their intellectual potential. Rather than sink into this quagmire of analytical complications and emotional cross-currents, we may say simply: We have no need of that hypothesis. That is, even if every group (or even every individual) had the same genetic potential, along with equal geographical backgrounds and equal cultural developments, differences in demographic characteristics alone would still make equality of performance virtually impossible. When demographic differences are instead added to other differences, the probability of equality of performance approaches the vanishing point. In addition, there are other reasons for doubting genetic explanations of intergroup differences.[15] Here, however, it is sufficient to say that we have no need of that hypothesis.

ECONOMIC CONSEQUENCES OF "EQUALITY"

Thus far, we have considered a few of the innumerable causes of inequality. We need to consider also some of the consequences of the concept of equality itself, especially where it is a pervasive and often passionate ideology applied to the real world. Among these consequences are difficulties in providing incentives for people to do their best work and dangers of even greater inequalities, both economic and political, as a result of trying to apply the vision of equality to the real world.

Pay Differentials

Among the economic consequences of the passionate pursuit of equality has been a reluctance or unwillingness of institutions or individual employers to pay employees doing the same job a pay differential sufficient to reflect the differences in productivity with which they perform the same duties. Merely a difference in the amount of supervision that employees require can be a considerable economic difference, even if the workers' own individually measured output is the same, since supervisory time is not free—and is in fact likely to be more expensive than the time of those being supervised. But, whatever the source of the differing value of particular employees to a business, letting one secretary be paid three times the salary of another secretary with the same duties is seldom feasible, for morale reasons, if nothing else. The same is generally true in many other occupations.

The net result is that attempts to reflect productivity differences with pay differences, in order to retain people who might be able to get more money elsewhere, often take the form of promotions, real or nominal. An outstanding secretary may, for example, be reclassified as an administrative assistant, while doing the same work as before. Such purely nominal promotions do less harm than genuine promotions which remove an employee from the job he performs in outstanding fashion to take on a new job which he may not perform as well, or even adequately.

"Redistribution" of Income

The "redistribution" of income is not only an ideological corollary of the passion for equality, it shares similar qualities of moralistic loftiness and analytical vagueness and confusion. As a Fabian socialist, George Bernard Shaw defined socialism as "a proposal to divide up the income of the country in a new way."[16] However, most income cannot be redistributed because it was not distributed in the first place. It is paid directly for services rendered and how much is paid is determined jointly by those individuals rendering the service and those to whom it is rendered.

This is obvious in the case of those who shine shoes or practice dentistry, but it is true also of those paid a salary for their work, rather than being paid separately for each given service rendered. Some income is in fact distributed, whether as Social Security checks, disaster relief aid, agricultural subsidy payments, or the like. But these are two very different processes, and the nature of those processes and their consequences must be understood before deciding to switch from one method of payment to another.

No one decides how much a shoe-shine boy or a dentist is "really" worth. In each case, the sum total of their fees is their income, after subtracting their respective costs. In short, each customer decides individually how much it is worth to him to have his shoes shined or his teeth fixed. No collectivized or political judgment is necessary. Thus the competition of the marketplace produces individual fees that add up to annual incomes not predetermined by anybody. Those who benefit directly from these services can determine how much the benefit is worth to them in each instance, rationing their usage according to the market price, their own pocketbooks, and the principle of diminishing returns (since few want their shoes or their teeth polished every day).

This more or less ideal type of market determination of incomes is modified, but not changed essentially, when people are employed at set salaries. Those more in demand, or less in supply, are likely to have their salaries set at higher levels. Moreover, those doing a better job are more likely to be retained during layoffs and down-sizing, and to receive promotions, real or nominal, and pay increases. In short, here too money is paid for services rendered by those directly benefitting and in accordance with the value of those services, as judged individually by those directly involved. Even in the case of salaried employees, income is not always determined solely by those salaries, as various income-earning options are often available after working hours, whether by moonlighting in the same field or some other, or by investing in various ventures from the stock market to real estate to writing the great American novel.

What all these various forms of market determination of income have in common is that the income is *not* distributed. It is directly earned in accordance with its value to others and in the light of competition from other available sources of the same services. To advocate a policy of income "redistribution" is to advocate not merely a change in statistical outcomes but a more profound change in the whole process by which people receive pay. The word "redistribution" is very deceptive insofar as it implies that we simply have distribution *A* today and should change to distribution *B* in the future. We are talking about collectivizing and politicizing the economic level of each individual. Such a massive institutional change should stand or fall on its own merits, not be quietly drifted into by soothing words or an innocuous prefix like "re-".

The idea that third parties can determine what someone's work is "really" worth involves not only incredible arrogance but intellectual confusion. The very fact that an exchange takes place at all is inconsistent with the existence of any "real" value that can be objectively discerned by anybody. Someone who pays a quarter for a morning newspaper does so because the value of the newspaper to him is greater than the value of the quarter. But the seller accepts the quarter only because the quarter is worth more to him than the newspaper. If there were any such thing as an objective value of a newspaper, one of these transactors must be a fool.

The same is true of any other transaction undertaken in a free market, whether what is being bought and sold are television sets or soybean futures. The medieval notion of a "just price," discernible by third-party observers, commits the same fundamental fallacy as "comparable worth" today. The hollowness of the pretentious formulas used in determining the latter is revealed when the relative rankings of the same occupations differ markedly from one jurisdiction to another. There is no "real" worth to compare and the arbitrariness of the process is revealed whenever different individuals operate independently and reach different results.

The economic problems likely to arise from having political or bureaucratic authorities determine people's income may be serious, but they are not half the story. A society in which some authorities can weigh millions of their fellow human beings in the balance, determine their worth, and unilaterally dispense their livelihoods as largess from the government is a profoundly different kind of society from that created and maintained in the United States of America for more than two centuries. As so often happens, a staggering political inequality can be created in the name of economic equality or social equity.

As with so many questions involving equality, the desired state of equality itself is not the real issue, especially since such a state of equality seems very unlikely to be achieved. What is crucial are the *processes* set in motion in hopes of approaching that state. To allow any governmental authority to determine how much money individuals shall be permitted to receive from other individuals produces not only a distortion of the economic processes by undermining incentives for efficiency, it is more fundamentally a monumental concentration of political power which reduces everyone to the level of a client of politicians. Even aside from what this means for freedom and human dignity, it makes virtually inevitable a constant and bitter struggle among all segments of the society for the favor of those who wield this massive power to determine each person's economic well-being. It is a formula for economic, political, and social disaster. Such power has, in a number of countries, led to a *nomenklatura* whose personal privileges have been a mockery of the very ideals of equality that led to such a concentration of power in pursuit of a mirage.

A question must also be raised as to how important—and to whom—it is to turn the whole economic and political system inside out, in order to produce numbers more pleasing to observers. Even some passionate advocates of equality have conceded that this is not an overwhelming concern of the general public. R. H. Tawney's landmark book, *Equality*, condemned the "violent contrasts" of economic inequality in England and the "sharp disparities of circumstance and education" to which they led, as well as other social evils he perceived—and yet he saw no groundswell among the English populace for equality. On the contrary, he declared that there was in England a "cult of inequality as a principle and an ideal," that inequality was "hallowed by tradition and permeated by pious emotions," that even the poor had a "tenderly wistful interest in the vacuous doings of the upper ten thousands,"[17] toward whom they should presumably be feeling bitter resentment instead.

More recently, Professor Ronald Dworkin has proclaimed that "a more equal society is a better society even if its citizens prefer inequality."[18] This is at least a tacit admission that issues of equality arouse no such passion in the general public as among the intelligentsia. That is one of the reasons why vast inequalities of political power must be created in pursuit of economic equality. The only sure winners are those who exalt themselves as the arbiters of the fates of millions.

"Equality" Promoting Inequality

The casual assumption that the ideology of equality in theory promotes a more equal society in fact is not only unproven but is a social time bomb. A more unequal and more embittered society can result instead.

One of the ways of promoting the ideology of equality is by defining various inequalities of performance out of existence. Thus cultural relativism refuses to classify some societies as civilized and others as backward or primitive. Whether comparing nations or subgroups within nations, cultural relativists proclaim all cultures and subcultures to be "equally valid" and entitled to "equal respect," as we "celebrate diversity." Immigrants, for example, are encouraged to continue speaking their foreign languages and preserving their separate cultures, while those black Americans who speak "black English" are likewise encouraged to continue to do so.

Cultures have consequences. Ignoring those consequences while proclaiming equality as a self-justifying ideal does nothing to benefit the less fortunate, and in fact tends to freeze them into their backward position while the rest of the world moves forward. The bitter irony is that all this philosophical self-indulgence widens the empirical gap in the name of narrowing it. Hispanics who speak Spanish earn lower incomes than Hispanics who speak English. Poor countries that cling to their cultural ways remain poor, while those that seize upon the things that produced wealth elsewhere tend to become wealthy themselves— Japan being the classic example. No nation was more painfully conscious of being technologically backward than Japan in the nineteenth century. That is what spurred them on to overtake the West. To have defined their backwardness out of existence would have been to condemn them to unnecessary poverty and thus to contribute to more economic inequality in the world than we have today.

While the children of affluent and well-educated parents can usually meet high educational standards better than the children of the less fortunate, lowering those standards, or discarding them completely, in the name of equality is likely to be especially harmful to the children of the poor and disadvantaged. Children from the homes of educated people with the money to afford books, computers, and other accessories of learning are likely to acquire much fundamental information and behavioral norms at home, even if both are neglected in their schools. It is the less fortunate for whom the public school classroom may be the only place in which they are likely to get the basic intellectual and social equipment that they will need for success as adults. Lowering the standards in the public schools may conceal disparities at the moment but is virtually certain to cause them to be greater in adulthood, at a point at which few can repair their deficiencies.

An even deadlier consequence of the quest for equality has been the development of a "non-judgmental" attitude toward beliefs and behavior. One of the most important social lessons of parents to their children in previous generations was to avoid people with bad behavior and not even to listen to them, for fear of being fatally misled. Today, schools not only spend more time on classroom discussions of social behavior, they do so non-judgmentally. This means that the ideas of delinquents and hoodlums are put on the same plane as the ideas of students raised to the strictest moral standards. Not only are the latter exposed to the ideas and experiences of the former, they are exposed in a setting where their overt rejection of such ideas and experiences would encounter the condemnation of the teacher. This is only one of many settings in which all people and all ideas are supposed to have "equal respect" so as not to threaten anyone's "self-esteem."

The only way to have "equal respect" is to have respect divorced from behavior and performance—which is to say, to have the word "respect" lose its meaning. One can dispense self-esteem as the Wizard of Oz dispensed substitutes for heart, courage, and brains. But printing any currency promiscuously destroys its value and there is no reason to doubt that the same principle applies to the currency of respect. Indeed, the transparent fraudulence of elaborate pretenses of respect are an added insult.

In a world where every society and every civilization has borrowed heavily from the cultures of other societies and other civilizations, everyone does not have to go back to square one and discover fire and the wheel for himself, when someone else has already discovered it. Europeans did not have to continue copying scrolls by hand after the Chinese invented paper and printing. Malaysia could become the world's leading rubber-producing nation after planting seeds taken from Brazil. Yet the equal-respect "identity" promoters would have each group paint itself into its own little corner, with its own insular culture, thus presenting over all a static tableau of "diversity," rather than the dynamic process of competition on which the progress of the human race has been based for thousands of years.

There is yet another way in which the mirage of equality promotes inequality in the real world. Ideological crusades in the name of equality promote envy, the principal victims of which are those doing the envying.

THE HIGH COST OF ENVY

Envy was once considered to be one of the seven deadly sins before it became one of the most admired virtues under its new name, "social justice." Under either name, it has costs as well as benefits. For some, envy can act as a spur to match the achievements or rewards of others currently more fortunate. This can happen in the case of individuals or in the case of whole nations, such as Japan, whose generations-long drive to catch up to the industrialized Western nations achieved success in the twentieth century. On the other hand, envy can also engender social strife, whose consequences include the possibility that the society as a whole can end up worse off, both materially and psychically, as a result of mutually thwarting activities, including mob violence and civil war. Among nations, a drive to achieve "a place in the sun" militarily can end in disaster, as happened to Japan in the Second World War and to Germany in both world wars.

The first kind of envy—the more or less natural and potentially beneficial envy that spurs self-development and achievement—creates few incentives for third parties to try to mobilize and heighten it for their own benefit. It is the second kind of envy, expressed in hostility toward others, that is useful for third parties pursuing careers as politicians, group activists, or ideologues. It is this kind of envy which can have high costs to society at large and to the poor especially. It is not simply that the poor may suffer psychically from having less than others and from being encouraged to dwell on their current situation, rather than concentrating on improving it. The very terms of the discussion encourage them to attribute their less fortunate position to social barriers, if not political plots, and so to neglect the kinds of efforts and skills which are capable of lifting them to higher economic and social levels.

Poorer Groups

For the currently less fortunate members of society, the costs of envy can be especially high when it misdirects their conceptions and energies. Where poorer people are lacking in human capital—skills, education, discipline, foresight—one of the sources from which they can acquire these things are more prosperous people who have more of these various forms of human capital. This may happen directly through apprenticeship, advice, or formal tutelage, or it may happen indirectly through observation, reflection, and imitation. However, all these ways of advancing out of poverty can be short-circuited by an ideology of envy that attributes the greater prosperity of others to "exploitation" of people like themselves, to oppression, bias, or unworthy motives such as "greed," racism, and the like. Acquisition of human capital in general seems futile under this conception and acquisition of human capital from exploiters, the greedy, and racists especially distasteful.

Often members of poorer racial, ethnic, or other social groups can acquire the needed human capital more easily from more fortunate members of their own respective groups than from others. However, the ideology of envy can also make their own more successful members suspect as "traitors"—and therefore also ineligible as either role models or direct sources of advice, skills, or other human capital. What such an ideology does essentially is paint the less fortunate into their own little corner, isolated from potential sources of greater prosperity. To the more fortunate, resistance or rebuffs to their attempts to help the less fortunate may be no more than a passing annoyance but, to the less fortunate themselves, this failure to acquire available human capital can be fatal to their own prospects.

Whole societies may remain mired in needless poverty, not only because envious visions have created a bogus explanation for their poverty that distracts them from readily available means of becoming more prosperous, but also because envy and fear of envy within these societies inhibit individual striving and innovation. Studies of many poor and primitive societies around the world repeatedly show the paralyzing effects of a pervasive fear of provoking envy among neighbors and relatives.[19] Long before Marxian or other "exploitation" theories arose, primitive peoples implicitly conceived of the world as a zero-sum game, in which the good fortune of some was the cause of the ill-fortune of others, whether in economic terms or in terms of health, love, or other benefits.

The cooperation and mutual trust necessary for many kinds of beneficial joint undertakings are more difficult to achieve within this cultural universe, however much such things may be taken for granted in more fortunate societies. Merely transferring capital or technology from these more fortunate societies is seldom sufficient to overcome the cultural handicaps of an envy-stricken society, especially when traditional beliefs are buttressed by more sophisticated modern versions of the envy vision spread by the Third World intelligentsia, often seconded by the intelligentsia in more fortunate countries.

The Dog in the Manger

The ultimate in envy is the dog in the manger. In one of Aesop's fables, a horse wants to eat some straw in his manger but a dog is lying on the straw. Although the dog does not eat straw, he refuses to move so that the horse can eat it, simply because he begrudges the horse the pleasure of eating the straw. The fact that this story has survived for thousands of years suggests that such attitudes are not unknown among human beings.

After the First World War, Romania acquired territory from the defeated Central Powers and these territories included universities that were culturally German or culturally Hungarian. At that point, roughly three-quarters of all Romanians were still illiterate, so the Germans and Hungarians at these universities were not keeping most Romanians from getting a higher education. Nevertheless, the government made it a priority to force Germans and Hungarians out of these universities. Moreover, when ethnically Hungarian students in Romania began going to universities in Hungary, the Romanian government forbad them to do so.

Such dog-in-the-manger attitudes are not peculiar to a particular country, race, or civilization. When Nigeria acquired its independence in 1960, many of the civil servants, professionals, and entrepreneurs in northern Nigeria were from tribes in southern Nigeria. One of the top priorities of the political leaders in the north was to force these southerners out of these occupations. Because of huge disparities in education, skill levels, and entrepreneurship, between the two regions of the country, there was no realistic hope of replacing southerners with northerners in any timely fashion. But northern political leaders were prepared to hire European expatriates in the interim, or to suffer a decline in the services formerly provided by the southerners, rather than suffer the blow to their egos of being so dramatically outperformed by their fellow Africans.

Similar attitudes existed halfway around the world in Malaysia, where discriminatory policies against the more educated, skilled, and entrepreneurial Chinese minority led many of them to leave the country. It was much the same story in the South Pacific, where the Fiji government's discrimination against the more educated, skilled, and entrepreneurial minority from India caused many of the Indians to emigrate.

Dog-in-the-manger attitudes are not confined to situations where there are ethnic differences. Tax policies are often shaped by a desire to "soak the rich," whether or not such policies are beneficial to the overall economy or even to the government's tax receipts. One of the most bitterly resented policies of the Reagan administration were tax-rate reductions referred to as "tax cuts for the rich," even though (1) tax rates in general were cut, (2) the government's tax *receipts* rose after the rates were cut and incomes rose, and (3) the upper-income brackets not only paid more total taxes than before, but even a higher percentage of all taxes. What was intolerable to critics was that "the rich" were able to pay these greater sums in taxes as a smaller percentage of their rising incomes. Estate taxes are an even clearer example of dog-in-the-manger attitudes, since they are a trivial proportion of total taxes collected by the government and it is questionable whether these taxes exceed the collection and compliance costs. But they serve the political purpose of striking a blow against inherited wealth.

The dog in the manger was elevated to the level of academic philosophy in John Rawls' *A Theory of Justice*, where policies that make society in general better off were to be rejected if they did not also make the poorest members of the society better off.[20] In other words, no matter how much any given policy might make vast millions of people better off, any small fraction of people at the bottom were in effect to have a veto over that policy. Even if those at the bottom were not made any *worse* off, no one else could be allowed to become better off without their participation. This is a particularly striking principle where there are low unemployment rates and many avenues of upward mobility, where those who do not choose to take advantage of these opportunities are to have their interests become pre-emptive as against the interests of the great majority of people who do.

These examples are merely particular illustrations of a more general set of attitudes which exalt envy and seldom count the cost of doing so. These costs include crimes of envy, where the purpose is neither to acquire someone else's possessions nor to avenge any loss of one's own, but simply to lash out against the "unfair" good fortune of another.[21] Such dog-in-the-manger crimes are often considered senseless or irrational but they are logical corollaries of the quest for cosmic justice.

Even those intellectuals who often attribute collective guilt for individual actions in other contexts—blaming American society for the assassination of President John F. Kennedy, for example—seldom apportion any part of the blame for crimes of envy to those like themselves who promote it.

Decision-Makers

Society as a whole can lose opportunities when people in various decision-making capacities have their decisions biased by envy. For example, a former admissions official at an Ivy League college warned prospective applicants not to say or do things that would reveal their educational or economic privileges, as that would tend to bias admissions officials against them. For example, she advised:

> The best thing you can do if you come from a privileged background is deemphasize it as best you can. For example, if you and your family took a ten-thousand-dollar vacation to Africa to go on Safari, it would probably be best not to write about it on your application. . . . It may rub admissions people the wrong way, since most do not have the money and resources to take such an exotic trip.[22]

Since the whole reason for having admissions committees in the first place is to select those applicants best able to make use of costly educational opportunities, envy here serves to undermine that goal when the decision-makers' biases are aroused against students who would otherwise be considered on their qualifications. Nor is this something confined to college admissions committees.

Similar reasoning has promoted educational policies which seek to create more equal outcomes for "special education" students with mental, physical, or psychological handicaps— again, with little or no regard for the financial costs of this to the taxpayers or the educational costs to other children in whose classrooms they are to be "mainstreamed," often with little regard to the disruptive effects of their special needs. These financial costs can be several times what it costs to educate the average student, while the educational results for a severely mentally retarded student may be imperceptible. The educational cost can also include a substantial part of a teacher's time being devoted to one or a few students, to the neglect of the majority. Yet, clearly, it is an injustice, from a cosmic perspective, that the minds and psyches of some are unable to cope with what ordinary students handle routinely. But just as some students suffer handicaps through no fault of their own, so can other children suffer from mainstreaming policies, likewise through no fault of their own.

It is also cosmically unjust that some students are born innately so unusually bright and/or have had such unusually favorable environments that they are capable of far higher levels of intellectual achievement than other children their age. One such student was able, in the fourth grade, to score higher than the average high school graduate on the mathematics portion of the Scholastic Aptitude Test. Yet the suggestion that he be given higher levels of mathematics to study than his classmates was rejected by the school principal, and this youngster was assigned the same fourth-grade mathematics as others, on grounds that it would be "a violation of social justice" if he were given higher levels of mathematics instruction.[23]

Nor was this principal unique. A member of a national commission on teaching mathematics opposed teaching computational skills because that means "anointing the few" who master these skills readily and "casting out the many" who do not, and urged that we throw off "the discriminatory shackles of computational algorithms."[24] More broadly, ability-grouping in different classes or in different schools is bitterly opposed by most public school officials on similar grounds. In short, both the mentally gifted and the mentally retarded are to be "mainstreamed" as part of the quest for cosmic justice—with little or no regard to the costs of this for the students, the taxpayers, or the society into which they are to go as adults.

Disregard of effects on third parties is also common on such issues as taxes, price controls, and law enforcement. Tax issues are not simply about whether one class pays more than another, but are also about the repercussions of particular kinds of taxes on economic development and national employment, which affect everyone. Price controls on food have often led to widespread hunger and malnutrition, as suppliers reduced their production and sales of food when this became unprofitable. Undermining law enforcement because of its perceived unfairness to the poor led to skyrocketing crime rates which hurt the poor worst of all.

Envy may cause many issues to be seen in terms of transferring benefits from *A* to *B*. But policies conceived of this way as transfers do not simply transfer. They change behavior in general and in fundamental ways. For example, price controls almost invariably lead to declines in the quantity and quality of what is supplied, to hoarding, and to black markets—whether the price that is being controlled is that of food, housing, gasoline, medical service, or other goods and services.

The point here is not simply that particular laws and policies have been counterproductive. The more fundamental point is that the whole invidious conception of policy-making spawned by envy is often deadly in its general effects on the society as a whole.

Authority and Differentiation
One of the most thoughtless and dangerous consequences of pursuing the mirage of equality and its accompanying envy has been a pervasive reaction against all forms of authority or even social differentiation. By authority is meant here the ability to get others to do things without either forcing them or convincing them. The classic example would be a physician who gives a patient a prescription to take, based on chemical, biological, and medical principles with which the patient is wholly unfamiliar. The patient simply relies on the physician's authority. Much of what children do is likewise based on their parents' authority. They learn the alphabet because their parents want them to, not because the children themselves understand the enormous ramifications of learning those particular 26 symbols in an arbitrarily specified order.

The mere sorting of people by such common titles as "mister" and "miss," and the differentiation of people by having adults address children one way and children address adults another, are all repugnant to many who pursue the mirage of equality. The practice of putting everyone—friends and strangers, young and old—on a first-name basis is one of the symptoms of this mindset. Much more serious are the systematic undermining of parental authority which can be found in public school textbooks and other materials which depict all sorts of moral and intellectual issues as things which each person must decide for himself or herself, not according to what has been taught by parents or by an always suspect "society."

It would be hard to imagine a more reckless gamble than encouraging youngsters with less than a decade of experience in the most elementary aspects of life to substitute that narrowly circumscribed experience, and their own undeveloped reasoning processes, for principles distilled from the experiences of millions of adults over generations of time. The child's own personal safety is often at stake in his willingness to respond to the imperative tone of a parent, in situations where there is no time to explain—or where the child does not yet have a sufficient background of experience to understand an explanation.

The verbal differentiation which reminds everyone of his own role—calling people "mother" and "father," instead of by their first names—or differentiation in dress, manner, or otherwise are all methods of establishing a social hierarchy that serves social purposes. But those to whom equality is an over-riding moral imperative see in all this only personal privilege and oppression. Yet authority may serve those who do not have it more than it does those who do. The parent who understands the underlying reasons for the things told to a child is benefitted less by authority than the child who does not understand those realities—and who needs to observe the cautions and apply the rules nevertheless. The specialized knowledge of the scientist, the physician, or the military commander is likewise used primarily to guide the actions of others who lack that knowledge and who would be much worse off to operate in ignorance. Authority is one of the ways of using the knowledge of some for the benefit of others.

Like everything human, authority is imperfect and subject to abuse, so it cannot be unlimited—and it is not. But to invoke the blanket slogan "Question Authority" is to raise the question: By what authority do you tell us to question authority? For authority to exist, there must have been some process by which particular people came to be regarded as more reliable guides than others. But there is no comparable process by which others come to be qualified to proclaim the dogma "Question Authority." Why should our skepticism be focussed on those who have already been through some testing and weeding-out process, and our trust be given to those who have not?

Authority is only one form of social differentiation. Even among people on the same social plane, various forms of address indicate differing levels of familiarity or intimacy, or differing levels of levity or seriousness as of a given moment. All of these things imply that social context matters, which is to say, that we cannot interact atomistically and ad hoc, without great costs and even dangers. Thus the same person may be "Mr. Smith," "Harry," "Daddy," "Lieutenant Smith," "Lefty," or "honey" in different contexts. Reminders of where we stand in relationship to different people are nothing more than admissions that we cannot play everything in life by ear without risking getting very badly out of harmony with others. All are made worse off without these verbal aids, and those most vulnerable are put at the greatest risk when the mirage of equality banishes such differentiation.

One of the most important social differentiations has now become passé and disdained—the distinction between the respectable poor and the disreputable poor. At one time, those who were poor could nevertheless take pride in their independence and self-sufficiency, even though they were at an economic and social level below that of the middle class. The respectable poor had the norms of society at large on their side, and the bad example of the disreputable poor as warnings to be used when they raised their children to be respectable people. Indeed, the children of the disreputable poor knew that their respectable neighbors were more highly regarded, thus providing incentives for some of these children to try to rise out of their position at the bottom of the social scale.

The welfare state, however, has made many of the respectable, self-supporting poor look like chumps, as the government has lavished innumerable programs on those who violate all rules and refuse to take responsibility for themselves. Now the incentives are reversed, tempting some of the respectable poor to take advantage of benefits available to those who are able to live without work, without saving for the future, and without even having to pay for a roof over their heads.

The Insatiability of Envy
Envy is insatiable in at least two different senses:

1. No conceivable redistribution of income, wealth, or other benefits will satisfy everyone, so there is no logical or political stopping-point in the process. Therefore the question is not which particular distribution is better or best, but whether the benefits of setting in motion a never-ending quest offers more potential for good or ill.

2. There is no unique and definitive rank-ordering of the innumerable advantages and disadvantages that individuals and groups may have simultaneously. Thus A can be envying B because of the latter's advantages while B is envying A because of the former's advantages.

Even in the simplest case, where both parties perceive A to have net advantages over B, redress is by no means always possible, quite aside from whether it is likely, or likely to be acquiesced in, by A. As a study of envy put it:

> The more one seeks to deprive the envious man of his ostensible reason for envy by giving him presents and doing him good turns, the more one demonstrates one's superiority and stresses how little the gifts will be missed. Were one to strip oneself of every possession, such a demonstration of goodness would still humiliate him so that his envy would be transferred from one's possessions to one's character. And if one were to raise him to one's own level, this artificially established equality would not make him in the least happy. He would again envy, firstly the benefactor's character, and secondly the recollection retained by the benefactor during this period of his erstwhile material superiority.[25]

The difficulties of satisfying envy under even these very simple and extreme conditions increase exponentially when there is no unambiguous way to say that A is better off than B in whatever dimension each values. Many parents, for example, are familiar with the situation in which each child thinks that a sibling is being treated better by the parents and therefore *each* has envy and resentment of the other or others. Nor can an objective third party, if one could be found, necessarily be able to declare which person has the net advantage when one is more fortunate according to one array of characteristics and possessions and the other is more fortunate according to another array of characteristics and possessions. Moreover, even in cases in which a third party regards A as clearly better off than B, it does not follow that either A or B will value and weigh the particular advantages and disadvantages the same way as this third party, much less the same as each other.

The crucial question is not whether reducing or eliminating envy is a desirable goal, any more than the question is whether cosmic justice is desirable. In both cases, the question is: What is the *cost* of promoting this goal? Insofar as reducing envy is attempted by purely intellectual means, such as showing how illogical or counterproductive envy can be, the costs are small and the results are likely to be correspondingly small. A more common and more costly way of attempting to deal with envy is by seeking political support for policies to reduce the disparities that promote it. However, in a democratic society, this effort must take the form of a public decrying of these disparities, as a prelude to seeking policies to reduce them. That means that this approach promotes envy in hopes of ultimately reducing it. One cost of this envious preoccupation that has already become a shocking sign of our times is the killing of children by other children over the possession of designer clothes, prestige trinkets, or other emblems of inequality. Envy is not cheap and its costs are not limited to material things.

FREEDOM VERSUS EQUALITY

Virtually no one seriously questions the principle of equal regard for human beings as human beings. No mother loves her baby any less because she knows that he does not have the capability of an adult. We may all agree on equality before the law and religious people can agree that we are all equal in the sight of God. It is the fatal step from equal regard to equal performance—or presumptively equal performance in the absence of social barriers—that opens the door to disaster.

We cannot all be equal as ballet dancers if some come from a cultural background where ballet dancing is highly prized and others come from a background where the very thought of becoming a ballet dancer is unlikely to occur to anyone. *Leaving out all questions of ability,* we still cannot be equal performers if we are not equally interested in the same kinds of performances. Women cannot be expected to have the same incomes as men if women's desires to have babies and care for them constrain their choices of careers and their continuity in a given career. Among the evidences that this is so is the fact that women who never married and who worked continuously since high school were earning more than men of the same description more than 20 years ago, before "gender equity" became a major legal issue.

One of the ways in which the dogma of equal performance is a threat to freedom is in its need to find villains and sinister machinations to explain why the real world is so different from the world of its vision. Courts of law condemn people for discrimination because the even or random distribution of people found in theory cannot be found in fact. The very thought of condemning the theory—or even testing it by evidence—seems unthinkable. If there are fewer women than men in engineering schools, then this is automatically assumed to be evidence that engineering schools discriminate against women. If this or that racial or ethnic group is "under-represented" here or there, this is considered virtual proof of racism.

Paranoia and freedom are an unlikely and unstable combination. If paranoia prevails, the right to be considered innocent until proven guilty cannot survive—and it does not survive in contemporary anti-discrimination laws, not to mention laws and policies on sexual harassment or child abuse. Similar paranoia in the anti-trust laws antedated current concerns about group discrimination by decades, and likewise destroyed the presumption of innocence, in very much the same way: Uneven statistics created a "rebuttable presumption" which often turned out in practice to be nearly impossible to rebut, regardless of what the truth might be.

A whole universe of the mind has already been created to explain inequality, as if equality were so natural and inevitable that its absence could only be explained by pervasive and sinister efforts against it. Thus all standards of behavior and performance are suspect as mere shams designed to ensure the continued advantages of the haves over the have-nots. Even efforts to help the less fortunate to acquire the behavioral prerequisites of productivity are often condemned as cultural imperialism, while the failure of the less fortunate to reap the rewards of productivity is also condemned as the fault of "society."

There has now been created a world in which the success of others is a grievance, rather than an example. Irrational as such ideological indulgences may be, they are virtually inevitable when equality becomes the social touchstone, for equality can be achieved only by either divorcing performance from reward or by producing equal performances. Since the latter is all but impossible, if only because everyone is not equally interested in the same kinds of performances, the passion for equality leads toward a divorce of performance and reward—which is to say a divorce of incentive and behavior, and even a divorce of cause and effect in our minds.

There is only so much divergence between prevailing theories and intractable reality that a society can survive. Yet theories of equality are unlikely to be re-examined—or examined the first time—when they provide a foundation for the heady feeling of being morally superior to a benighted "society." The demonizing of those who do not share the prevailing social assumptions and ideological passions among the intelligentsia has made discussion all but impossible on a growing range of issues. For example, those who believe in systemic processes— the marketplace, traditional values, constitutional law— designed to convey the desires and preferences of the many, rather than the special visions of the few, are suspected, accused, or defined as spokesmen for economic privilege, out to thwart the political achievement of equality.

Such bogeyman visions of the social universe are utterly heedless of such facts as the widespread belief in the intrinsic equality of people among the leading figures in the traditions commonly identified as "conservative."[26] Despite their own clear and unequivocal statements, those opposed to grand schemes of politically imposed equality have been widely depicted as being opposed to equality itself and as being apologists for privilege. That the proponents of such grand schemes are so little constrained by facts, or by any need to check facts, and so willing to people the world of their mind with demons is one symptom of a larger recklessness, with larger dangers for the whole society.

What is crucial here is not simply that the apostles of politically imposed equality wish to see a certain kind of world, but that they are heedless of what their efforts are doing to the real world around them. Indeed, their presumptions of moral superiority, and the moral exhibitionism that so often accompanies such presumptions, make reconsideration in the light of evidence a particularly painful process, correspondingly less likely to be engaged in. Economic inefficiencies and the crippling of the educational system by the passion for equal rewards without equal results are just some of the costs of this approach. Poisonous relations between the races and the sexes, or between those who simply happen to disagree philosophically, are other high costs of this crusade. Internal dissensions and demoralization have played a crucial role in the decline and fall of other civilizations, and there is no reason to expect this one to be immune.

III

~

The Tyranny of Visions

Lenin surrounded himself with official publications, and works
of history and economics. He made no effort to inform himself
directly of the views and conditions of the masses . . . He never
visited a factory or set foot on a farm. He had no interest in the
way in which wealth was created. He was never to be seen in
the working-class quarters of any town in which he resided.

—PAUL JOHNSON

III

The Tyranny of Visions

V. I. Lenin represented one of the purest examples of a man who operated on the basis of a vision and its categories, which superseded the world of flesh-and-blood human beings or the realities within which they lived out their lives. Only tactically or strategically did the nature of the world beyond the vision matter, as a means to the end of fulfilling that vision.

Lenin, Hitler, and Mao were the pre-eminent twentieth-century examples of leaders who sought to adjust people to visions, even when that entailed the deaths of millions of human beings. Lenin's preoccupation with visions was demonstrated not only by his failure to enter the world of the working class, in whose name he spoke, but also by his failure to ever set foot in Soviet Central Asia—a vast area larger than Western Europe, and one in which the doctrinaire and devastating schemes of Lenin and his successors would be imposed by force for nearly three-quarters of a century.

Visions are not inherently dogmatic. Einstein's vision of the universe was at least as revolutionary in science as Lenin's was in politics. Yet Einstein insisted from the outset that his theory of relativity must be checked against observable facts before it could be accepted—and so it was, by scientists around the world, including those scientists who were initially skeptical, but who became convinced by the evidence of their own experiments.

The more sweeping the vision—the more it seems to explain and the more its explanation is emotionally satisfying—the more reason there for its devotees to safeguard it against the vagaries of facts. Cosmic visions are more likely to be cherished in this way, whether these are visions which explain society and history by racial superiority (as with Hitler) or by class struggle (Marx, Lenin) or by some other grand simplicity that is cosmic in its scope. Visions of cosmic justice are just one variety of cosmic visions. Hitler's cosmic vision was quite different from anything conceived by John Rawls.

Cosmic visions of society are not just visions about society. They are visions about those people who hold these visions and the role of such people in society, whether these people are deemed to be leaders of a master race, the vanguard of the proletariat, saviors of the planet, or to have some other similarly self-flattering role as an anointed visionary group "making a difference" in the unfolding of history. Heady cosmic visions which give this sense of being one of the anointed visionaries can hold tyrannical sway in disregard or defiance of facts. This becomes painfully apparent, whether we look at visions of war and peace or at social visions.

VISIONS OF WAR AND PEACE

There are two diametrically opposed theories of how best to prevent war. One is that of military deterrence, involving acquiring both weapons and allies, and based on arousing the public to the dangers from aggressor nations. The other theory is that disarmament agreements and mutual peace pacts among potential enemies, along with a de-escalation of hostile rhetoric, is the way to prevent war.

Will Rogers gave perhaps the most succinct account of the deterrence theory:

> We better start doing something about our defenses. We are not going to be lucky enough to fight some Central American country forever. Build all we can, and take care of nothing but our own business, and we will never have to use it. Our world heavyweight champion hasn't been insulted since he won the title.[1]

Believers in this theory acquire no sense of moral superiority, even in their own eyes, though they obviously regard their method of preserving peace as more effective in practice. However, believers in the opposite theory—disarmament—not only regard their own method of preserving peace as more effective, their sense of moral superiority is apparent when they declare themselves to be "anti-war," part of "the peace movement," and use other terms which strongly suggest that the differences between themselves and those with opposite views are due to their being devoted to peace, while others are either warlike or not as committed to peace as themselves, if not venal mouthpieces for military industries.

As liberal editor Oswald Garrison Villard put it in the 1930s, opposition to disarmament was a matter of "militarism, backed by all the rich and privileged, by every opponent of a new and better world."[2] Historian Charles A. Beard was one of many who depicted rearmament as a ploy of the military industries, reflecting "the interests of cupidity" among "armor-plate manufacturers," or "munition-makers" and the like.[3] Bertrand Russell said in 1936 "a sinister interest helps to manufacture warlike feeling as well as munitions."[4] John Dewey likewise spoke of "the arms and munitions by which the merchants of death wax fat and bloated."[5]

In other words, as far as the disarmament advocates were concerned, there was not even an honest disagreement as to the best way to preserve peace. During the later Cold War era, Bertrand Russell returned to the same themes, referring to those who supported nuclear deterrence policies as people who "belong to the murderers' club." He described British Prime Minister Harold Macmillan and American President John F. Kennedy as "the wickedest people that ever lived in the history of man" and as "fifty times more wicked than Hitler" because he saw their promotion of nuclear deterrence as "organizing the massacre of the whole of mankind."[6]

While this air of moral superiority has been a consistent element in the disarmament approach to preserving peace, it has not played any such role among those with the military deterrence approach. The greatest apostle of the military deterrence approach during the 1930s, Winston Churchill, said later in a eulogy to the man whose foreign policy he had so often criticized then as dangerously mistaken, Neville Chamberlain:

> The only guide to a man is his conscience; the only shield to his memory is the rectitude and sincerity of his actions. It is very imprudent to walk through life without this shield, because we are so often mocked by the failure of our hopes and the upsetting of our calculations; but with this shield, whatever the fates may play, we march always in the ranks of honour.[7]

This asymmetry in presumptions of moral superiority is centuries old and by no means confined to different theories of preventing war. On issue after issue, the morally self-anointed visionaries have for centuries argued as if no honest disagreement were possible, as if those who opposed them were not merely in error but in sin.[8] This has long been a hallmark of those with a cosmic vision of the world and of themselves as saviors of the world, whether they are saving it from war, overpopulation, capitalism, genetic degradation, environmental destruction, or whatever the crisis du jour might be.

Given this exalted vision of their role by the anointed visionaries, those who disagree with them must be correspondingly degraded or demonized. On issues of war and peace, opponents who prefer deterrence to disarmament are often depicted as intellectually deficient, lacking in imagination, or blinded by habit. John Dewey, for example, depicted those who disagreed with the 1920s movement for an international renunciation of war, such as led eventually to the Kellogg-Briand treaty of 1928, as people exhibiting "the stupidity of habit-bound minds."[9] In other words, it was not even possible for others to have weighed the probabilities of this untried approach differently. According to Dewey, only "mental inertia"[10] could explain why some people were not willing to gamble their national security on international renunciations of war. Their reasons, Dewey said, "are psychological rather than practical or logical"[11] or else the arguments against the renunciation of war "comes from those who believe in the war system."[12]

Differences on issues of war and peace are associated with fundamentally different visions of the world, which produce different beliefs about a whole constellation of social and political issues.[13] For example, a believer in the welfare state or in socialism is less likely to prefer the theory of military deterrence than is a believer in laissez-faire economics, judicial restraint, and other aspects of the opposite vision.

John Dewey, for example, was opposed to "laissez-faire" economics and to a "punitive" approach to the criminal, which enables us to ignore "our part in creating him."[14] Bertrand Russell supported the idea of "social justice between nations and between individuals," which would require that "all ultimate ownership and control of land and raw materials must be in the hands of the international authority," for "private property, in regard to raw materials, involves gross injustice and a powerful incentive to war."[15] Like many others on the political left, he advocated schools in which there is "as little discipline as is compatible with the acquisition of knowledge, and no corporal punishment whatever."[16] In short, pacifism is part of a coherent vision that extends well beyond issues of war and peace, while deterrence is part of a very different vision that is also coherent in its larger sweep.

Here, as elsewhere, the question as to which method of avoiding war in fact tends to produce the desired result and which turns out to be counterproductive receives remarkably little empirical examination from the anointed visionaries. It is the *quest* for peace, like the quest for cosmic justice, that exalts them morally—irrespective of whether their strategy actually reduces the dangers of war or even increases those dangers. Here, as in other expressions of cosmic visions, results are not the test. Taking a moral stand is the test, as economist Roy Harrod discovered at a 1934 rally of the British Labour Party. A Labour Party candidate proclaimed that Britain ought to disarm "as an example to others"—a very common argument at that time.

> 'You think our example will cause Hitler and Mussolini to disarm?' I asked.
> 'Oh, Roy,' she said, 'have you lost all your idealism?'[7]

Personal exaltation, not empirical consequences for other people, has long marked cosmic visions and their advocates, however much they may proclaim their love of humanity, peace, the environment, the poor, or other ostensible beneficiaries of their activities.

While those with the opposite vision—advocates of military deterrence—typically see other human beings as rational decision-makers like themselves, and accordingly seek to present potential aggressor nations with sufficient counter-force to deter military action, those with the cosmic vision of the anointed visionaries are more likely to define the problem psychologically as hostile emotions and irrational behavior that may get out of hand and thereby lead to war. This second and more psychological explanation casts the visionaries in a superior—almost therapeutic—role as they seek to "relieve international tensions," to dispel "misunderstandings" through more contact with both the leaders and the peoples of adversary nations, and to portray these potential enemies as "human beings like ourselves." Two of the great conflicts of the twentieth century—first between the Western democracies and the Nazis and then between the Western democracies and the Communists—both illustrate this pattern, which can be seen in the events that led up to World War II and in the events of the later Cold War.

The Road to World War II

During the period between the two world wars, the terms of the competition between deterrence theories and disarmament theories were very uneven within the Western democracies. The latter vision was clearly in the ascendancy, both in theory and in practice. While the policies and statements of British Prime Minister Neville Chamberlain epitomized this conciliatory approach in the years that led up to World War II, that vision was pervasive in Britain before he ever achieved that office and it was a political force to be reckoned with in the United States and in other Western democracies.

Accordingly, a whole series of international disarmament agreements and mutual security conferences and agreements marked the two decades between the world wars. As in other contexts, the actual specifics of the disarmament agreements received remarkably little critical scrutiny by the morally anointed visionaries, who welcomed these treaties' symbolism and their presumed psychological efficacy in relieving international tensions. For example, one of the earliest of these disarmament pacts, the Washington Naval Agreement of 1922, inhibited the growth of British and American navies but presented no practical barrier to the growth of Japan's navy, since the permissible limits on Japan were no less than Japan's current capacity to build warships—and, after the point was reached when the treaty limits would have become a practical barrier, Japan simply ignored the agreement, as Nazi Germany would later ignore a similar naval treaty with Great Britain.[18]

The inherent asymmetry of disarmament treaties between democratic and despotic governments—violations by the latter being far less constrained by public opinion or even public knowledge—were glided over by disarmament advocates.

The Washington Naval Agreement was followed by a series of much-heralded international conferences at Locarno (1925) and Lausanne (1932), among other places, spawning such euphoric phrases as "the spirit of Locarno" and declarations that the Lausanne conference had "saved Europe" and opened "a new era" for the world.[19] The same euphoria would later greet Neville Chamberlain's famous pronouncement after the Munich conference of 1938 that there was now "peace in our time."

In the vision of the disarmament advocates, armaments themselves are the enemy. "Away with rifles, machine guns, and cannon!" cried France's foreign minister, Aristide Briand,[20] co-author of the Kellogg-Briand Pact of 1928 renouncing war. Bertrand Russell in 1936 declared, "disarmament and complete pacifism is indisputably the wisest policy" and urged "the gradual disbanding of the British army, navy and air force."[21] This was not an isolated individual opinion but one echoed in Parliament. British Labour Party leader Clement Attlee declared, "We on our side are for total disarmament because we are realists."[22] While the British government did not disarm, its expenditures on its military forces, which had declined from the late 1920s to the early 1930s, rose much less than those of Nazi Germany in the years leading up to the outbreak of the Second World War in 1939.

There was a similar pattern in the United States, where the American army had less than a quarter of a million men and was only the sixteenth largest army in the world, behind the armies of Greece and Portugal. Moreover, even this skeletal force lacked enough military equipment to go around. Some

American soldiers had to train with wooden rifles and with mock-ups of tanks and cannon. Probably no great nation in all of history was so completely disarmed as the United States. Nevertheless, even the modest military spending of this era was attacked by those who considered themselves part of "the peace movement." In a 1936 article in *The Atlantic Monthly* titled "We Militarize," Oswald Garrison Villard dismissed "bogies as to our 'coming' war with Japan."[23] Perennial Socialist Party presidential candidate Norman Thomas declared: "A prospective victory by Hitler over most of Europe is highly unlikely."[24]

Nor were such sentiments confined to the intelligentsia. They found echoes in the Congress of the United States. Influential Senator Gerald Nye, for example, denounced "the new insane armament race," and declared that "the masses of Japan are no more desirous of a conflict with the people of the United States than our own citizens are desirous of a war with the people of Japan." But, even if war came, Japan "couldn't get within several hundred miles of our shore" and "neither could we get within striking distance of the Japanese coast."[25] A whole literature of this era argued that war fears were being whipped up by military suppliers, the "merchants of death" in the phrase of the time. In short, those who advocated military deterrence were not even granted the small dignity of being honestly mistaken, much less any possibility of being right.

The irrelevant argument that the *people* of various countries did not want war proved to be as politically indestructible as it was fallacious as an indicator of what the *governments* of those countries were likely to do. This same argument was repeated on many occasions on the other side of the Atlantic by British Prime Minister Neville Chamberlain, and was to re-surface a generation later during the Cold War and be repeated innumerable times once again, as if it were a new and deep insight. In September 1938, Chamberlain spoke of "the desire of the German people for peace,"[26] less than a year before the most catastrophic war in history was unleashed by Hitler. Similarly, Chamberlain spoke of "the passionate desire of the Italian people for peace,"[27] which was no doubt equally true and equally irrelevant to Mussolini's actions.

Like many others during the years between the two world wars, Chamberlain warned of the dangers of an "arms race"—what he called "this senseless competition in rearmament which continually cancels out the efforts that each nation makes to secure an advantage over the others."[28] This echoed what Bertrand Russell had said in 1936, that "every increase of armaments by one Power is met by an increase on the other side, which requires a further increase by the first Power."[29] Such neutral assessments from above the struggle—a favorite position for anointed visionaries—overlooked two crucial facts in the life-and-death decisions that have to be made about military preparedness.

First of all, an obviously aggressive nation, such as Nazi Germany during the 1930s, launches a military buildup in order to accomplish its goals by force or the threat of force, while those who build up counter-force are seeking to avoid being attacked or forced into surrender. If a defensive military buildup—an "arms race"—fails to secure any net advantage whatever against the aggressor, it is nevertheless a huge success if it prevents aggression or the need to surrender. From the standpoint of the non-aggressor nation, it is not trying to *gain* anything at the expense of anybody else, but simply recognizes the grim reality that military preparedness is part of the price of maintaining the peace, independence, and freedom that it already has.[30] If military deterrence permits that to be done without bloodshed, it is not a "waste" because the arms are never used, but instead is a bargain because they were formidable enough that they did not have to be used, nor lives sacrificed in the carnage of war.

The anti–"arms race" argument often also includes the *post hoc, ergo propter hoc* fallacy—in this case, that arms races lead to war because wars often occur after contending nations have built up their military capacity.[31] Empirically, it is certainly true that, as nations see the prospect of war approaching, they tend to arm themselves. This can hardly be surprising. Nor does it indicate the direction of causation.

Implicit in all this is the self-congratulatory notion that other people are behaving irrationally and that one's own superior understanding and virtue are the answer. From here it is but a short step to the therapeutic approach of seeking to manage other people's emotions, assuming that wars occur because those emotions get out of hand, rather than because some political leaders deliberately choose courses of action that threaten evil consequences for others because those same actions seem to offer good prospects for themselves in the form of territorial aggrandizement, political glory, and the like.

To those with the opposite vision, this all looks radically different. If one assumes that other human beings are basically rational, like oneself, then potential aggressors—whether international or ordinary criminals at home—can be expected to calculate the prospects of success and to be more inclined to take a chance where one's potential victims are weakest. From this perspective, arming potential victims reduces the dangers of aggression and especially of successful aggression.[32] But this approach offers no special role for those who presume themselves to be morally superior.

Another fallacy in the "arms race" argument is that, like so much else in the vision of anointed visionaries, it overlooks the intractable economic reality of scarcity. No country has the unlimited resources implied in the argument that an unending upward spiral of armaments will ensue. Moreover, some countries will reach their economic limits before others.

In a later era, President Ronald Reagan understood this very clearly when he explained to a horrified group of *Washington Post* journalists that he intended to win the arms race with the Soviet Union, because American resources greatly exceeded those of the U.S.S.R., so that Soviet leaders would ultimately be forced to the bargaining table to begin reducing their threatening nuclear arsenal and scale back their international aggressions. To the equal disbelief and disdain of many, he likewise said on more than one occasion that we were seeing the last days of the Soviet Union,[33] which could not take the combined strains of their own counterproductive economic system and foreign military adventures. The fact that events proved him right has done absolutely nothing to rehabilitate President Reagan in the eyes of those to whom evidence has never been more important than the vision on which their own egos depend.

In the years between the two world wars, as in other eras, the argument that military preparedness meant a wasteful arms race was supplemented by the argument that war is futile. As Chamberlain put it, war "wins nothing, cures nothing, settles nothing."[34] This long-standing staple of pacifists, like many other self-congratulatory pronouncements, has almost never been subjected to any empirical examination.

If war is so futile, why then were there tears of relief and gratitude when the peoples of Western Europe were liberated from their Nazi conquerors by the invading Allied armies and when those in slave labor camps and extermination camps were freed? Was it futile to occupy a defeated Germany and Japan, rooting out their centuries-old traditions of militarism that had brought such terror and havoc to their neighbors? Was the American Civil War futile in freeing millions of human beings from slavery? The "futility of war" is an exhilarating set of sounds rather than a serious statement to be tested seriously against facts. Some wars are indeed futile. Some are not. Sweeping *a priori* pronouncements on the subject serve little purpose other than self-exaltation.

Along with the military disarmament of the interwar years went a moral disarmament. Despite the savagery in word and deeds of the Nazis in Germany and the warlords in Japan, Chamberlain again epitomized the spirit of the times in speaking neutrally of "both sides" as if there were some moral equivalence. Thus he spoke of Japan's brutal and unprovoked invasion of China as "the outbreak of hostilities" there and "the unhappy conflict" that ensued.[35] During periods of friction between Nazi Germany and Great Britain, he called for "restraint and toleration by the Press of both countries."[36] Hitler's orchestrated violence through manipulation of the ethnic Germans in Czechoslovakia's Sudetenland was referred to as "a succession of serious incidents in the unhappy Sudetenland" and later Chamberlain spoke of "the present controversy" there and condemned "extremists on both sides."[37]

These were not clarion calls, from either a moral or a self-defense point of view. In such a climate of opinion, where war itself was seen as the enemy, widespread opposition to military preparedness was hardly surprising. At Oxford University, students pledged never to fight for their country—a pledge that spread to other students at other universities. Bertrand Russell declared: "The purpose is peace, and the way to achieve it is to say: *We will not fight.*"[38] Pacifism was strong in the United States as well. France, as the country nearest to Germany, was better armed but, as Churchill noted in 1932: "France, though armed to the teeth, is pacifist to the core."[39]

At the heart of the spiritual disarmament behind the military disarmament was the cosmic vision of anointed visionaries. Both the rhetoric and the foreign policy of British Prime Minister Neville Chamberlain reflected virtually every aspect of that vision. First, there was the therapeutic vision of war, that "if you want to secure a peace which can be relied on to last, you have got to find out what are the causes of war and remove them."[40] Among these causes were "misunderstandings,"[41] "grievances, differences and suspicions"[42] and other psychological problems such as "enmities"[43] and "an atmosphere of ill will."[44] Given this therapeutic vision of the causes of war, Chamberlain's incessant repetition of the theme that "personal contacts"[45] between heads of state were the way to dissipate this psychological malaise and defuse emotions was perfectly consistent.

We now know that Hitler and Mussolini developed contempt for Chamberlain, as a result of the prime minister's willingness to fly repeatedly to meet with them—they never flew to England to meet with him—even under humiliating conditions. Nor was this contempt an incidental sidebar to history. The Axis powers risked war with countries whose military potential they fully understood to be greater than their own, because they did not think that these countries had the guts to fight or the good sense to build up sufficient military forces in time to fight effectively.

Contempt for the weak-kneed leaders and timid policies of the Western democracies were essential parts of that calculation which led the dictators to unleash war. Yet, at the time, little of this was understood in the West beyond the ranks of a very few like Winston Churchill, who was then a back-bencher in Parliament, alienated from his own party and often an object of disdain and ridicule, when he was noticed at all.[46] By contrast, when Chamberlain prepared to fly to Munich for his historic meeting with Hitler in 1938, he left amid tumultuous cheers and applause and the virtually unanimous support of all parties in the House of Commons—and was similarly welcomed back with great acclaim in Parliament and in the country, as he proclaimed "peace in our time."

Both the material and the moral disarmament of the West were crucial to their vulnerability to attack by nations whose military potential was not as great, but who counted on having a decisive series of victories before the democratic nations could build up their armaments and their resolve. This Axis strategy came dangerously close to success.

A stunning, swift, and unbroken series of major military victories by the Axis powers dominated the first half of World War II, whether in Europe, Asia, or North Africa. Poland and France fell to the blitzkrieg of the Nazi armies in a matter of weeks, and Norway was overrun in a matter of days. The Japanese swept down across Southeast Asia to capture the Philippines, Malaya, and the East Indies after bombing Pearl

Harbor. When the British finally won a battle in North Africa near the end of 1942, Winston Churchill declared frankly, "We have a new experience. We have victory."[47] The war was already three years old at that point. The only miscalculation of the Axis powers was in believing the Western democracies incapable of continuing to fight the war for years, in the face of repeatedly devastating defeats, retreats, and mounting casualties.

Whether this would have been a miscalculation a generation later, at the time of the Vietnam war, is another question. But, in World War II, once the Western countries, and especially the United States, finally mobilized their resources—which supplied not only their own military forces but also those of the Soviet Union—the tide turned as decisively in their favor in the second half of the war as it had been in favor of the Axis powers in the first half. Nevertheless, despite an overwhelming victory at the end, the Allies were desperately close to defeat earlier. When Winston Churchill was appointed prime minister of Britain in May 1940, he said in reply to his chauffeur's congratulations: "I hope that it is not too late. I am very much afraid that it is. We can only do our best." He had tears in his eyes.[48]

This desperate moment came for Britain and the world, not because the West lacked the material resources to defend itself, or because the Axis enemy did not know of the West's superior military potential, but because that potential was allowed to remain mere potential for decades, while the aggressors were visibly and rapidly arming, not only materially but in spirit, while the West was disarming materially as a result of disarming in spirit.

At the end of the war, Churchill looked back and said: "There never was a war in all history easier to prevent by timely action than the one which has just desolated such great areas of the globe."[49] But such timely action to deter war with armaments and military alliances, as Churchill had urged throughout the 1930s, would not have exalted the anointed visionaries, as their championing of opposite policies did. The British, American, and other Allied soldiers who paid with their lives in the early years of the war for the quantitatively inadequate and qualitatively obsolete military equipment that was a legacy of interwar pacifism were among the most tragic of the many third parties who have paid the price of other people's exalted visions and self-congratulation.

The Cold War

In the years immediately following the end of the Second World War, there was a keen awareness in many quarters that the West's weak and foolish policies had led to the horrors of that war—and had risked even greater horrors had that war been lost. As *Time* magazine said in its May 14, 1945, issue:

> This war was a revolution against the moral basis of civilization. It was conceived by the Nazis in conscious contempt for the life, dignity and freedom of individual man and deliberately prosecuted by means of slavery, starvation and the mass destruction of noncombatants' lives. It was a revolution against the human soul.[50]

A generation whose young men had fought, suffered, and died on innumerable battlefields around the world now clearly understood the need for military alliances to deter aggression. Nor was this either a political party issue or an ideological issue in the United States, except on the far left. Mainstream liberals like Harry Truman and Hubert Humphrey supported the North Atlantic Treaty Organization and military deterrence in general. President John F. Kennedy declared, "we dare not tempt them with weakness." However, even at the beginning of the Cold War, disarmament advocates who again called themselves "the peace movement" opposed military expenditures and military alliances, and used many of the same arguments and much of the same rhetoric that pacifists had used to such fatal effect in the years leading up to World War II. However, such movements and such arguments were crushingly defeated politically in the United States, though they were much more formidable in Europe, which has generally been to the left of the U.S. on both domestic and foreign issues.

The great turnaround came with the Vietnam war, which lasted longer than the Second World War and showed no sign of victory or even a stalemate that would put an end to the mounting casualties. Now the discredited ideas of a previous generation enjoyed a resurgence, especially among those too young to have suffered the bitter lessons that had destroyed similar illusions before.

Demands for "summit meetings"—the new term for what Chamberlain had so often called "personal contacts"—and for disarmament agreements once more became politically irresistible. Once again, the actual substance of these meetings and the verifiability of agreements that grew out of them were considerations swamped by the euphoria they produced. The "spirit of Locarno" and of other sites of international meetings in the years between the two World Wars were now echoed in "the spirit of Geneva," "the spirit of Tashkent," and of many other sites of Soviet-American meetings of heads of state.

This approach reached its zenith (or nadir) in the Carter administration and its failure was epitomized by President Carter's expression of shock when Soviet troops invaded Afghanistan. Carter began to repair the neglect of American military forces but it was, in the tragic phrase of the early years of World War II, "too little and too late." General disenchantment with both the domestic and foreign policies of that administration brought the most profound change in American policies at home and abroad in many years with the election of Ronald Reagan in 1980.

While the public was ready for the change, the morally anointed among the intelligentsia and the media clearly were not and expressed both alarm and disdain as President Reagan began a military buildup to counter the growing Soviet nuclear arsenal and proposed exploring the prospects of an anti-missile defense system to reduce the effectiveness of the Soviet nuclear threat. Perhaps the peak of this new trend that Reagan set in motion came with American military action in the Persian Gulf war of 1991, when the much-lamented military spending of the 1980s paid off under the Bush administration when abundant, high-tech military equipment led to a swift victory with remarkably few American casualties, despite many dire predictions of a bloodbath on the battlefield.

Another change of administrations, as a result of the 1992 elections and due more to domestic than to international developments, brought yet another return to the de-emphasis of the military and a resurgence of international conferences and summit meetings—and of the illusions on which they are so often based. These illusions were perhaps epitomized in a *New York Times* headline about the 1997 visit of China's President Jiang Zemin to the United States, where there were said to be "signs of bonding" between the two presidents.[51]

SOCIAL VISIONS

If the tyranny of visions can prevail in questions of war and peace—which is to say, life-and-death questions for both individuals and societies—it should hardly be surprising that the same tyranny can prevail in visions of social and economic activity. Perhaps no vision underlies more social and economic theories than the vision of the rich robbing the poor, whether in a given society or among nations. The belief that the poor are poor *because* the rich are rich is reflected in such expressions as "the dispossessed" or "the exploited," as well as in more elaborate theories ranging from Marxism and Lenin's theory of imperialism to modern "dependency theory."

Can people who have never possessed be dispossessed? Can they be plundered for riches they never had? The assumption of some prior, more fortunate condition also seems to underlie Edwin Markham's poem, "The Man with the Hoe," which paints a bitter and tragic picture of a man bent with toil, whose mind and soul are numbed with weariness:

> How will you ever straighten up this shape;
> Give back the upward looking and the light;
> Rebuild in it the music and the dream . . . ?

Similar assumptions of better times in the past underlie a whole literature on the "noble savage" or romantic pictures of pre-industrial times in Europe. In particular places and times, there have indeed been retrogressions and there have also been such things as the Spanish looting of the treasures of the Incas, but the more general explanation of wealth differences in this way, domestically and internationally, would require more evidence that this was a pervasive pattern. As with so many other examples of cosmic visions, the intellect of the intellectuals has not been bent toward *testing* such beliefs against empirical evidence, but rather toward *illustrating* such theories with selected facts.

If the goal were to test the belief that the wealth of the wealthy derives from the poverty of the poor, then one might, for example, see if countries that abounded in millionaires and billionaires had poorer people than countries that do not. Alternatively, one might see if a particular period in a country's history when the rich were getting richer was also a period when the poor were getting poorer. More sophisticated tests would also be possible—but only if testing were the goal.

Among nations, it would be possible to see whether the acquisition of colonies led to an accelerated enrichment of the imperialist nations and whether the loss of such colonies led to economic setbacks in the imperialist nations and/or an improved prosperity among the liberated peoples. Yet remarkably little attention has been paid to such empirical questions by those with cosmic visions of exploitation. One of the masterpieces of propaganda has been Lenin's *Imperialism,* which brilliantly illustrates his theory with statistics, without subjecting it to the slightest test.

Lenin's Imperialism

The achievement that Lenin's *Imperialism* represents as a masterpiece of propaganda cannot be fully appreciated without first understanding the formidable obstacles its author had to overcome, in order to rescue Marxian economic theory from more than half a century of history that contradicted it—and *then* launch the rescuing theory in the face of masses of additional evidence contradicting Lenin's own doctrine as well.

Marx's theory of the end of capitalism depended crucially on the working class' responding to a deterioration of its condition—whether absolute deterioration or deterioration relative to other classes—by becoming revolutionary.[52] Within Marx's own lifetime, the idea of absolute impoverishment of the working class was abandoned by Marx and Engels themselves, who noted the growing prosperity and subjective embourgeoisement of the proletariat around them in England.[53] By the time Lenin wrote *Imperialism,* the Marxian predictions were well on their way to becoming a joke. How could Marxism be rescued in the face of an increasingly prosperous and quiescent working class in the capitalist world? On a more practical level, how could a new vision inspire new revolutionaries to risk all in a bid to seize political power? Lenin's *Imperialism* solved both these huge problems.

The "exploitation" of the working class in capitalist nations was ameliorated and revolution postponed, according to Lenin, by their sharing in the fruits of the exploitation of less developed countries. In search of this exploitation, industrial nations sent to less developed foreign countries their "surplus" capital that would otherwise have created the serious economic problems at home that Marx had envisioned. In Lenin's words, the new capitalists "plunder the whole world" and, out of their "enormous *super-profits*" they are able to bribe the more fortunate members of the domestic working class and, in particular, their leaders who are co-opted.[54] Thus "millions of toilers" now "live in more or less bourgeois conditions of life," Lenin said.[55] In this way, capitalist imperialism simultaneously keeps the working class quiet and finds outlets for a "prodigious increase of capital, which overflows the brim."[56]

Lenin offered not only an excuse but a vision, presented as an empirically testable hypothesis, for which he proceeded to offer empirical evidence. The key evidence in *Imperialism* was presented in a table like that below.[57] The countries listed in capital letters across the top are European industrial nations that are making capital investments abroad. The places listed vertically on the left-hand column are the destinations of this capital.

BILLIONS OF MARKS, CIRCA 1910

	GREAT BRITAIN	FRANCE	GERMANY	TOTAL
Europe	4	23	18	45
America	37	4	10	51
Asia, Africa, and Australia	29	8	7	44
TOTAL	70	35	35	140

Before examining the implications of this table, we must first recognize that it fulfills one of the important functions of propaganda: It *appears* to offer evidence, and certainly it offers information, on a subject that most people are unlikely to be familiar with and in numbers on an impressive scale—in this case, billions of marks. Modest as this achievement might seem, from a purely logical standpoint, it was well suited to its purpose. As someone knowledgeable about confidence games has pointed out, the purpose of the confidence man is not to convince skeptics but to help others to believe what they already want to believe. Displaying the paraphernalia of evidence, embellished with appropriate rhetoric, accomplished that important purpose.

From the standpoint of logic, evidence differs from mere facts in that evidence consists of facts more consistent with one theory than with another. Therefore the appropriate criterion for evidence is not simply whether it is factually accurate but whether it is logically relevant to making that discrimination. Parading statistics which document to the hilt things that are not at issue—that capitalist industry was growing greatly and that banks had huge deposits,[58] for example—is logically vacuous. Nevertheless, it can and did succeed as propaganda designed to create an atmosphere of great knowledge about esoteric things and their presumably sinister inner meanings.

Returning to the table, opposite, the data for Britain seem on the surface to fit Lenin's theory of imperialism, since Britain had relatively little invested in Europe, as compared to its investments in the presumably less industrially developed regions of the world. However, the data for France and Germany seem to fail even this superficial test. As regards Britain, Lenin said: "The principal spheres of investment of British capital are the British colonies, which are very large also in America (for example, Canada) not to mention Asia, etc." Thus "enormous amounts of capital are bound up most closely with colonies." A substantial part of France's European investments were said to be in Russia, a less developed part of Europe at that time, and

Germany's foreign investments were said to be "divided fairly evenly between Europe and America."[59] But no data were presented in support of any of these claims. Nevertheless, Lenin's argument seems at first to be reasonably plausible and reasonably consistent with his theory of imperialism as a means of exporting capital from the industrial to the non-industrial world, where greater and more profitable "exploitation" is presumably possible.

What is remarkable, however, if not astonishing, are the huge and heterogenous categories in which data for the investment recipients are presented. "America," for example, encompasses the entire Western Hemisphere, which includes levels of economic development ranging from the Amazon jungles to the steel mills of Pittsburgh. Similarly, "Asia, Africa, and Australia" are three whole continents lumped together as one category, likewise covering regions that range from jungles to industrial metropolises. For those who wish to believe, the presumption is that capital is being exported to the less developed regions of these vast and heterogenous territories—and, for this constituency, that is sufficient.

For those who do not share Lenin's vision, or those who retain some fundamental respect for logic and evidence, a finer breakdown of data would make the whole Leninist construction collapse like a house of cards. For the period covered by Lenin's data and doctrine—the late nineteenth and early twentieth centuries—the United States was the leading recipient of British, German, and Dutch capital.[60] At the time when Lenin wrote, the British Empire was the largest empire in the world, encompassing one-fourth of the earth's land and one-fourth of the world's population. Contrary to Lenin, however, its investments did not go primarily to its imperial possessions. Its greatest investments were in another industrial country, the United States, which received more British investments than all of Asia or all of Africa or all of Latin America.[61]

Britain's other major overseas investments were also in European offshoot societies and economies in Australia, Canada, Rhodesia, and South Africa.[62] Nor was Britain unique in this pattern. France and Germany were likewise reluctant to sink much of their money into Africa, for example,[63] and commercial trade with Africa was similarly trivial for the economies of the European imperial powers.

On the eve of the First World War, Germany exported more than five times as much to a small country like Belgium as to its own colonial empire,[64] which was larger than Germany itself. France likewise exported ten times as much to Belgium as to all its vast holdings in Africa, which were larger than France. Out of Germany's total exports to the world, less than one percent went to its colonies in Africa.[65] During the period when Lenin wrote, and for much of the remainder of the twentieth century, the United States invested more in Canada than in all of Asia and Africa put together.[66]

In short, the huge and heterogenous categories used in Lenin's *Imperialism* concealed evidence that showed the direct opposite of what this classic work of propaganda claimed. The idea that the non-industrial world offered a safety valve outlet for the "surplus" capital of the industrial world cannot stand up if the industrial nations are investing primarily in each other. This would be adding to their economic and social pressures, rather than relieving them, if the Marxian theory of excess capital accumulation were correct.

The utter failure of Lenin's *Imperialism* as a work of logic only highlights its success as propaganda. To convince people of the truth of something that is true by logical inference from evidence requires no talent whatever in the arts of propaganda. But to convince many highly educated people around the world of a theory that is demonstrably false, by the use of hard data, artfully presented, is clearly a triumph of propaganda and makes Lenin's *Imperialism* one of the great classics of that art.

Marxism-Leninism is the ultimate in a common pattern among intellectuals with cosmic visions—highly sophisticated defenses of primitive misconceptions. In this case, the misconception is that the rich are rich *because* the poor are poor—that what is involved, in one way or another, is that wealth is extracted from the many for the benefit of the few, whether among classes or among nations. This might make sense if wealth were a zero-sum game, but that such theories could flourish in an era when the total wealth of the human race has been increasing at a rate unprecedented in the history of the species is both a triumph of propaganda and a symptom of something in the human psyche that makes it susceptible to such a picture.

To accept the opposite view—that some have become dramatically better at producing the wealth made possible by modern technology, and that others lag in applying this technology—is to threaten the psyches of those who lag and deprive their would-be rescuers of a dramatic and historic role. It is no denigration of the genius of propaganda to say that it flourishes in a particular context. So do all other achievements.

Did Lenin himself believe the argument he presented in *Imperialism*? In light of his many other cynical words and deeds, it is doubtful. What is crucial, however, is that he was committed to a vision. As Joseph Schumpeter said, "The first thing a man will do for his ideals is lie."[67] As history has also shown, especially in the twentieth century, one of the first things an ideologue will do after achieving absolute power is kill. That too is part of the tyranny of visions.

Social Reform

Not only sweeping theories but also more limited reform movements can reflect cosmic visions. More specifically, reform movements often reflect the vision of cosmic justice—opposition to a situation deemed morally intolerable, regardless of whether the reform makes those trapped in that situation better off or worse off. For example, reformers shocked by housing conditions in the slums or working conditions in the Third World have often banned by law the housing conditions which offended them or used import bans or public vilification to keep American firms from importing the products of labor working under conditions that offend American reformers.

In the great age of housing reform—the late nineteenth century in the United States—conditions in the slums were truly appalling. Most of the people living in northern urban slums at that time were immigrants, many from much poorer countries than the United States and themselves much poorer than most Americans. These immigrants lived packed into small, ill-ventilated apartments, often three or more per room. If they were lucky, they all shared a toilet out in the hall. If not, they had to go outside—regardless of the weather—to an outhouse in a back yard. In short, there is no question that the conditions were far worse than in slums a hundred years later and far worse than conditions that anyone would like to see human beings living in. To the reformers, it followed as the night follows the day that laws should ban such conditions and set standards for the way apartment buildings were built, as well as standards for how much space must be allowed per person and other desirable features that all housing must have.

Nothing is easier than to agree with these reformers that it was unjust, in some cosmic sense, that some people should find themselves forced to live so much like animals. However, some slum-dwellers were not financially incapable of getting better housing but were living in overcrowded and run-down buildings as a way to skimp and save money to send to their families back in Europe, either for food and shelter or to buy tickets to come join them in America. Some families saved money in order to prepare a better future for themselves and their children. Crusading reformer-journalist Jacob Riis, while painting a heart-rending picture of the slums in which Jewish immigrants were living on the lower east side of New York, noted in passing their small earnings, "more than half of which goes into the bank."[68]

In short, people were making choices and trade-offs, however appalling those choices might seem to observers—and however "unfair" it might be that such choices had to be made in the first place, when so many others had so much better options available to them. The kinds of reforms being promoted in the nineteenth century did not expand the slum-dwellers' options but reduced them. Since better housing mandated by law cost more money, immigrant slum-dwellers now had to devote a higher percentage of their incomes toward purchasing more expensive housing with features that would be more pleasing to third-party observers, rather than make the trade-offs that they themselves would have preferred with their own money.

When one considers the dire poverty and dangers to life and limb from mobs that Jews were facing in Eastern Europe at the time, the desire of Jews on the lower east side of New York to get their loved ones fed and then brought over to America clearly had an urgency, however much that fact might be unknown or ignored by housing reformers. Nor was the desire to save for a better future for their children merely a forlorn hope, as the later rise of Jews in the United States showed.

The fact that people were literally starving to death in the streets of Ireland during the potato famine of the 1840s likewise lent urgency to the desire of Irish immigrants in America to get their families moved across the Atlantic. With the Irish, as with the Jews, most immigrants crossed the ocean with their passages paid by members of their respective groups living in America. So did many people from other immigrant groups. Some of the worst housing conditions were endured by Italian men, living up to ten to a room and sending money back to their families in Italy.

Reformers who reacted to the slums before their eyes, and to their own sense of social injustice, had nothing to force them to face the trade-offs inescapably faced by the people living in those slums. Even the fact that slum-dwellers often joined with slum landlords to physically resist being evicted by the authorities from housing declared "sub-standard" did not cause Jacob Riis or many other reformers to reconsider whether what they were doing was really in the best interests of the people whose interests they were ostensibly protecting. It is all too easy for people with more formal schooling to believe that they know better than those directly concerned.

It is equally easy for others, a hundred years later, to say complacently that "in the long run" it was better for these slums to disappear, so that housing reform was a success, after all. Indeed, reformers at the time often made "before" and "after" comparisons of the housing in which people lived, concluding that these reforms had made those people better off. Yet both comparisons stop far short of proving what they imagine that they prove.

The underlying problem was the poverty of the people living in the slums. Their housing was only a symptom of that problem—indeed, one of the ways of minimizing the effects of their poverty, by leaving more money to meet their needs for food, for help to relatives abroad, and to prepare for their children's rise in American society. Housing reform added nothing to these people's meager incomes. On the contrary, it commandeered some of those meager resources to make third parties feel better.

We need not wonder whether nineteenth-century slums would have persisted indefinitely without housing reform crusades. Nineteenth-century crusaders paid no such attention to the housing of Southern blacks and yet that housing improved in a generation at least as much as the housing in Northern immigrant slums. As blacks acquired more options through rising incomes, their housing improved accordingly. There is no reason to believe that immigrants were incapable of doing the same thing. Indeed, rising incomes among immigrants and their children often led them to acquire housing of an even higher standard than the minimum prescribed by the laws passed by housing reformers.

Much the same story can be told today of reformers who decry "sweatshop labor" in Third World countries that export their products to the United States to be sold by American stores. Nothing is easier than to take cheap shots at those stores for "exploiting" Third World people—and nothing will hurt those Third World people more surely than losing one of their few meager opportunities to earn incomes by producing at lower costs than more fortunate people in more industrialized nations. Imposing American wages or American working conditions on people who do not have American productivity means pricing many of those people out of a job. It is reducing their options, rather than adding to those options.

Like so much that is done in the quest for cosmic justice, it makes observers feel better about themselves—and provides no incentives for those observers to scrutinize the consequences of their actions on the ostensible beneficiaries. As in other cases, human beings are sacrificed to the tyranny of visions because those sacrificed are not the same as those exhilarated by the vision.

SUMMARY AND CONCLUSIONS

Visions are inescapable because the limits of our own direct knowledge are inescapable. The crucial question is whether visions provide a basis for theories to be tested or for dogmas to be proclaimed and imposed. Much of the history of the twentieth century has been a history of the tyranny of visions as dogmas. Previous centuries saw the despotisms of monarchs or of military conquerors, but the twentieth century has seen the rise of ruling individuals and parties whose passport to power was their successful marketing of visions. Almost by definition, this was the marketing of the *promises* of visions, since performance could not be judged before achieving the power to put the vision into action.

In countries fortunate enough to have democratic means of replacing the representatives of visions that failed, these visions could be replaced by very different visions, as happened in Britain and the United States in the 1980s. But the most dramatic and far-reaching visions of the twentieth century—the totalitarianisms of the left and right—permitted no such reversals, short of war or revolution. Yet, even in democratic nations, a prevailing vision can survive many setbacks and even disasters. The prevalence and power of a vision is shown, not by what its evidence or logic can prove, but precisely by its *exemption* from any need to provide evidence or logic—by the number of things that can be successfully asserted because they fit the vision, without having to meet the test of fitting the facts.

How often has it been asserted, for example, that opposing ideas may have fit "earlier and simpler times" but no longer apply to the "complexities" of the present—without the slightest evidence being asked or given to show that earlier times were in fact simpler, without a single step of logic to show that opposing ideas were more applicable then than now and, most important of all, without ever bringing any alternative set of ideas simultaneously to the test of either facts or reason?

Among the perennially popular notions for which evidence is neither asked nor given, most prove to be very self-flattering to those who believe them. For example, it was for many years a popular staple among American liberals that the Roosevelt New Deal "saved capitalism" in spite of itself—that is, in spite of the capitalists who opposed FDR and his programs. In other words, the stupid or short-sighted businessmen were going to destroy themselves if it had not been for the far-sighted liberals in Washington who saved them and the economic system that made their success possible.

Could anything be more self-congratulatory? Yet, despite the innumerable times that this thesis has been repeated in the media and in academia, it would be virtually impossible to find any serious attempt to advance either evidence or a structured argument to prove it. Since the American economy always recovered from all previous depressions, the case that it recovered from the depression of the 1930s because of the Roosevelt policies is far from obvious. Indeed, what was peculiar about the depression of the 1930s was how long it lasted—and here a case can be made, and in fact has been made, that the constant economic experiments in Washington under FDR generated an atmosphere of uncertainty—and that this uncertainty impeded economic recovery,[69] as uncertainty has impeded economic prosperity in countries around the world and in many periods of history. The point here is not to claim that this thesis is the right one—just that it uses evidence and logic, as the prevailing vision does not and does not have to.

Powerful visions may not only dispense with facts, they can defy the most blatant facts for years on end. For the better part of the twentieth century—or, rather, for the worst part of the twentieth century—people by the millions fled countries viewed favorably by the intelligentsia to go to countries viewed unfavorably by the intelligentsia. Subjecting theories to the rigors of logical scrutiny and empirical verification may be tedious, but subjecting whole populations to the fancies of intellectuals and politicians has repeatedly proved deadly. That lesson has been written in blood across the history of the twentieth century and surely the time is overdue to read it.

Even in countries fortunate enough to escape the ideological totalitarianism that engulfed hundreds of millions of human beings in this century, grandiose economic and social experiments created hunger in countries that used to export food and turned great cities into scenes of both physical and moral squalor that their own citizens fled.

It might be thought that the emphasis placed on visions here is either misplaced or exaggerated because many things that are said and done politically are motivated by narrow self-interests, either by the self-interest of the individual politician or that of the politician's financial or political backers. The extent to which politics is a conflict of special interests, rather than a conflict of visions, can be debated. However, even when what is involved is fundamentally a matter of special interests, often there is a clash with opposing special interests and the net outcome may well depend on the extent to which either side can enlist wider political support. Here the general climate of opinion, including the prevailing vision that forms the background for many people's opinions on particular issues, can be decisive.

Whether political leaders say what they do out of conviction or as a matter of expediency matters little to this argument. What will be expedient for a particular individual depends on what others sincerely believe. Even lies are effective only because they are regarded as the truth. It is precisely this prevailing sense of what is true and what is right—the vision—that determines what will be expedient for those who are untroubled by either consideration.

While it is convenient to refer to visions in terms of the assumptions they embody and the theories to which they lead, as well as the specific hypotheses that follow from those theories, not everyone systematically analyzes visions in this way. In fact, one of the important advantages of a prevailing vision is that it is so easily and unconsciously absorbed from those around us, without our having to take the trouble to think about it. A prevailing vision is, in computer terms, the "default setting" for our opinions on a whole spectrum of issues. It is what we believe in general when we have no special reason to believe otherwise.

Most people have neither the time nor the inclination to delve deeply into theories and evidence, much less the expertise to do so effectively. Indeed, even experts in particular fields may have little time or inclination to put to the test a vision that extends far beyond their field. In our own specialty, we may have learned through experience or analysis just how false the prevailing vision is as regards a particular issue in that field but, when we turn to things outside our own area of special knowledge, the easiest thing is to accept what "everybody" assumes. For example, if we have studied the actual effects of rent control in countries around the world, then we are unlikely to believe arguments for making housing "affordable" in this way, but we may remain susceptible to other arguments, based on the prevailing vision, that food, medical care, or other things should be made "affordable" by similar government action.

So natural and almost inevitable does the prevailing vision often appear that, when we encounter someone who is clearly out of step with this vision, it is all too easy to dismiss his views on one issue by referring to other issues in which he is also out of step with the vision. Thus, his views on national health insurance may seem suspect or not to be taken seriously because "What can you expect from someone who is against affordable housing for the poor?" In short, intellectual consistency becomes something to condemn when it is consistency with a different set of assumptions than those embodied in the prevailing vision. Put differently, the prevailing vision not only does not require evidence, it becomes a substitute for evidence in condemning alternative views, so that the real criterion is not which theory better fits empirical facts but which theory better fits the prevailing vision.

Visions are not inherently dogmatic and the social sciences are not inherently unscientific in their methods. To explain the levels of dogmatism and resistance to facts found in too many writings in the social sciences—and still more so in the humanities and in the popular media—it is necessary to explore what purposes are served by these visions, by their evasions of particular evidence, and—especially in the case of the humanities—by their denigration of the very concepts of evidence and cognitive meaning. Similarly, not only are particular achievements denigrated, the very concept of achievement is denigrated by being downgraded to "privilege," not only as regards people but also as regards writings that have earned the respect of successive generations of readers, but which are now referred to as "privileged writings" and treated as no more worthy of special attention or study than the popular culture of the moment or alternative writings more ideologically in tune with the times.

Just as ancient tyrants gave the people bread and circuses, in exchange for their loyalty, so visions can acquire a tyrannical sway over people's minds by offering them an exalted sense of themselves in exchange for their loyalty to the vision through all the vicissitudes of facts to the contrary. This self-exaltation can take many forms on many issues.

Whether the particular issue is crime, automobile safety, income statistics, military defense, or overpopulation theories, the one consistency among them is that the conclusions reached exalt those who share the vision over the great unwashed who do not. What is most self-exalting is taking a position above the contenders, creating "moral equivalence" between aggressor dictatorships and defensive democracies or between animal species and human beings. With criminal law issues, theories of "root causes" of crime tend to put criminals and "society" on the same moral plane by depicting crimes as the fruits of society's failings. In short, moral equivalence—whatever form it takes—is moral self-exaltation. It would be expecting quite a coincidence for the theories and policies which best serve this personal purpose, for those with this vision, to also best serve others for whose ostensible benefit these theories and policies are proposed.

How little the well-being of the ostensible beneficiaries really matters is shown by how little attention is usually shown to testing theories logically beforehand or empirically afterwards, as compared to the unremitting efforts put into propagandizing or into demonizing those with alternative views. As an economist described someone who passionately advocated particular economic policies, without the most elementary knowledge of economic analysis and with little or no concern for empirical consequences, "he asks not whether it is water or gasoline he is tossing on the economic fire—he asks only whether it is a well-intended act."[70]

Similarly, some of the most passionate opponents of the American involvement in the Vietnam war, ostensibly on grounds of the sufferings of the Indochinese peoples from the military conflict there, were not nearly as concerned about the

137

fate of these peoples after the Americans left. As two former 1960s radicals said of their comrades who remained radicals:

> Their moral amnesia allowed them to ignore the fact that more Indochinese people were killed in the first two years of the Communist peace than had been killed on all sides in a decade of the anti-Communist war.[71]

While many opponents of the Vietnam war on humanitarian grounds (myself included) were also horrified later by the vast and traumatic exodus of the "boat people" fleeing the new regime in Vietnam, and still more so by the genocide carried out by the victorious Communist regime in Cambodia, those who opposed the war from the perspective of an ideological vision created no such uproar over the sufferings of the peoples of Vietnam, Cambodia, or Laos after the Communist victories in Indochina. As with so many other issues, *the fate of the ostensible beneficiaries was never an over-riding consideration,* if it was a consideration at all. Long before the Vietnam war, the fates of other ostensible beneficiaries had been repeatedly brushed aside with phrases about "the growing pains of a new society" or "You can't make omelettes without breaking eggs." It was the vision that mattered, not the flesh-and-blood human beings who were viewed as the incidental casualties of the vision.

The crucial role of self-exaltation underlies the way that those with opposing opinions are viewed. It is not sufficient, for example, to depict those who believe in preserving peace through military deterrence as mistaken, factually incorrect, illogical in their analysis, or dangerous in their conclusions. All of these things, even if true, would still leave them on the same moral plane as the anointed visionaries and would leave both subject to the same requirements of evidence and logic, as their arguments are laid before others to decide. What is necessary, from the standpoint of self-exaltation, is to depict proponents of military deterrence as not "really" being for peace, as being either bloodthirsty or acting as venal representatives of special interests who desire war for their own ends.

In much the same way, it has not been enough to claim that advocates of judicial restraint are mistaken in their premises or conclusions. They must be depicted as calloused toward the less fortunate, biased against women and minorities, and otherwise morally unworthy. The verb "to Bork" has been added to the language by one of the most extensive demonization campaigns of this sort.

Self-exaltation introduces a bias into considerations of many issues. For example, it creates a vested interest in the incapacity of other people. That is, there is not only a tendency to see people as helpless and not responsible for their own actions, there is a tendency toward policies and programs which in fact reduce them to that condition and induce them to accept that image of themselves, while the anointed visionaries play the role of rescuers. This is only one of the ways in which the vision of morally anointed visionaries ministers to the egos of the anointed, rather than the well-being of the ostensible beneficiaries of their efforts.

The almost universal disdain toward the middle class—the bourgeoisie—by those with cosmic visions can be more readily understood in light of the role of such visions as personal gratification and personal license. The middle classes have been classically people of rules, traditions, and self-discipline, to a far greater extent than the underclass below them or the wealthy and aristocratic classes above them. While the underclass pay the price of not having the self-discipline of the bourgeoisie—in many ways, ranging from poverty to imprisonment—the truly wealthy and powerful can often disregard the rules, including laws, without paying the consequences. Those with cosmic visions that seek escape from social constraints regarded as arbitrary, rather than inherent, tend to romanticize the unruliness of the underclass and the sense of being above the rules found among the elite.

Rules, traditions, and self-discipline all represent guidance from the distilled experiences of others, rather than self-indulgence based the inner light of one's own vision. It is almost axiomatic that those with cosmic visions must disdain the bourgeoisie. The visionaries must also disdain the kind of society that evolves over the generations through experience, rather than the kind of society that can be created by the imposition of an inspired vision.

Self-exaltation is *not* inherent in all theories or all visions. For example, theories of *laissez-faire* economics, such as those of Adam Smith in the eighteenth century or Friedrich Hayek in the twentieth, do not create a vision of a morally anointed elite and, in fact, both writers said that men differ less than dogs.[72] Hayek in particular went out of his way to praise the good intentions of his opponents and to say that the dire consequences he expected from their activities were the furthest things from the humane objectives they were seeking.[73]

The arrogant vision of an anointed elite comes not from the simple fact that it is a vision, but from the sense of themselves as morally anointed among those who hold this particular vision. That vision makes that particular belief possible and therefore becomes a vision which its devotees are loath to relinquish, even in the face of evidence against the views that sustain their exaltation. Desperately ingenious efforts to evade particular evidence, or to denigrate objective facts in general, are all consistent with their heavy emotional investment in their vision, which is ostensibly about the well-being of others but is ultimately about themselves.

It is not visions, as such, that are inherently dangerous. What is dangerous are *insulated* visions. Nothing produces insulation from reality more effectively than power and money. Power means that decisions based on the prevailing vision over-ride others' decisions, beliefs, or evidence, regardless of what the facts may be. Money means that support for the ideologically preferred conclusions can be purchased not only from "hired guns" but also by funding the research and writings of those committed to the same viewpoint, for whatever reasons, while those who disagree are left unfunded.

While the tyranny of visions reached its height (or its depth) in twentieth-century totalitarian regimes, the long, costly, painful—and ultimately successful—struggles against those regimes did not end the tyranny of visions. That tyranny has now become part of Western democratic nations themselves. Indeed, the drive to impose that tyranny ever more widely in the United States has led to trends which can only be called the quiet repeal of the American revolution.

IV

The Quiet Repeal of the American Revolution

By the rude bridge that arched the flood,
Their flag to April's breeze unfurled,
Here once the embattled farmers stood
And fired the shot heard round the world.

—RALPH WALDO EMERSON

The Revolutionary War for American independence was not simply a landmark event in the history of the United States. It was a landmark in the history of the world—and especially a landmark in the history of the evolution of free and democratic societies. Its international significance was symbolized by France's donation of the Statue of Liberty to the United States on the one hundredth anniversary of the Declaration of Independence and by the creation of a facsimile of this statue in China, more than a century after that, by protesters vainly seeking to create a free and democratic government in that country.

The American revolution was in some ways the most far-reaching of all the great revolutions in history. Other revolutions may have had more sweeping rhetoric, or greater extremes of violence and terror, or more categorical *claims* of change. They may even have had more radical changes of personnel, as in the change from czarist to Communist rulers in Moscow, while replacing one form of autocratic despotism with another and more bloody form.

The American revolution, however, went further in rejecting a basic conception of man and society that goes back thousands of years, and which is still with us today. Down through the centuries, people of the most diverse philosophic persuasions have proceeded as if what was needed was to replace false doctrines with true doctrines and false leaders with true leaders — the heathens with the faithful, capitalists with socialists, royalty with republicans, and so on. But, unlike the French revolution or the Bolshevik revolution, for example, the American revolution and its resulting constitution did not center on a change in the cast of characters in high places or on a change in their political language or immediate policy agenda. Its central concern was in establishing new *processes* by which whoever occupied the places of power could be restrained and replaced. In short, it did not pretend to have a doctrinal truth but instead implied a deep skepticism that anyone had either a monopoly on doctrinal truth or such moral or intellectual rectitude as to be exempt from constraints, condemnations, or dismissals from office by their fellow men.

What the American Constitution established was not simply a particular system but a process for changing systems, practices, and leaders, together with a method of constraining whoever or whatever was ascendant at any given time. Viewed positively, what the American revolution did was to give to the common man a voice, a veto, elbow room, and a refuge from the rampaging presumptions of his "betters." That is why it was not simply a national phenomenon but has been seen by others in the world at large as a landmark in the general struggle for human freedom.

That is also why it must be opposed by those with more ambitious visions — *even if they do not consciously feel any animosity against constitutional freedoms* — because, on issue after issue, those freedoms stand between the morally self-anointed and the realization of dreams which have overwhelming importance to them. Some of these dreams revolve around the quest for cosmic justice, in which constitutional constraints may be seen as technicalities to be finessed. Other dreams may be about personal ambitions that can be fulfilled only in a very different kind of society from that established by the Constitution of the United States. Ego and ideals are of course not mutually exclusive but may readily exist in the same individual, who may even mistake the former for the latter.

A quarter of a century before he delivered the Gettysburg address, Abraham Lincoln gave another speech, much less celebrated but all too relevant to our theme and our times. In an 1838 address in Springfield, Illinois, Lincoln asked where future dangers to the freedom and security of the American people might be found. It was not from foreign enemies, he said, but from internal threats. If and when the fundamental principles and structure of American government should fall under attack, "men of sufficient talent and ambition will not be wanting to seize the opportunity" and "strike the blow" against free government.[1]

What is particularly significant about Lincoln's warning is that it was based on a vision of what human beings are like, and especially what talented and ambitious leaders are like. To Lincoln, the historic achievement of American society in establishing a new form of government in the world was in jeopardy from later elites precisely because that achievement was already history:

The field of glory is harvested, and the crop is already appropriated. But new reapers will arise, and *they*, too, will seek a field. It is to deny, what the history of the world tells us is true, to suppose that men of ambition and talents will not continue to spring up amongst us. And, when they do, they will as naturally seek the gratification of their ruling passion, as others have so done before them. The question is, can that gratification be found in supporting and maintaining an edifice that has been erected by others? Most certainly it cannot.[2]

While the ambitions of some might be satisfied with "a seat in Congress, a gubernatorial or a presidential chair," Lincoln said, *such belong not to the family of the lion, or the tribe of the eagle.*" He added:

What! Think you these places would satisfy an Alexander, a Caesar, or a Napoleon?—Never! Towering genius disdains a beaten path. It seeks regions hitherto unexplored.—It sees not *distinction* in adding story to story, upon the monuments of fame, erected to the memory of others. It *denies* that it is glory enough to serve under any chief. It *scorns* to tread in the footsteps of *any* predecessor, however illustrious. It thirsts and burns for distinction; and, if possible, it will have it, whether at the expense of emancipating slaves, or enslaving freemen.[3]

That some leader dangerous to the basic institutions of American society would arise, Lincoln thought inevitable. Safeguarding those institutions would require a public sufficiently united, sufficiently attached to freedom, and sufficiently wise, "to successfully frustrate his designs."[4] Today it would also require a public sufficiently resistant to incessant criticisms and condemnations of their society for failing to achieve cosmic justice. Moreover, if the dangers in our own times were limited to those of "towering genius," there would be much less danger than there is. However, all that is needed are towering presumptions, which are increasingly mass-produced in our schools and colleges by the educational vogue of encouraging immature and inexperienced students to sit in emotional judgment on the complex evolution of whole ages and of vast civilizations.

Political leaders are not the only ones with a vested interest in opposing the existing framework of American society, precisely because it *is* the existing framework, so that supporting it offers no paths to the kind of glory they seek. The intelligentsia have exactly the same incentives as Napoleonic politicians, even if the glory they seek is not necessarily direct political power in their own hands, but only the triumph of their doctrines, the reordering of other people's lives in accordance with their visions, a display of their own intellectual virtuosity, or simply a posture of daring in the role of a verbal dandy. The easiest way to achieve all these goals is to disdain the beaten path, as Lincoln put it, and to attack or undermine the fundamental structure of the American political system and society.

A small but all too typical example was provided by a Stanford law student serving in one of the many organizations devoted to "prisoner's rights." She said, "It's precisely because prisoners are viewed as the castaways of our society—that's what draws me to them even more." She added, "We should want to know why a person can't function in this society, what it is about this society."[5] In this formulation—common among the intelligentsia—people are in jail because they *cannot* function *in this society.* It is not that they do not *choose* to function, but to prey on others instead, and to commit acts that are crimes in all sorts of societies around the world. Usually neither evidence nor logic is asked or given for such blanket indictments of "society" or for a non-judgmental view of criminals. It is simply part of the zeitgeist and a shortcut to distinction—cheap glory—to take a stand against "society."

Unfortunately, what many call "society" is in fact civilization. No one is openly opposed to American civilization, nor even covertly plotting its demise. Many of those pursuing a vision of cosmic justice simply take an adversarial position against traditions, morals, and institutions that make the survival of this civilization possible. The prerequisites of civilization are not an interesting subject to those who concentrate on its shortcomings—that is, on the extent to which what currently exists as the fruits of centuries of efforts and sacrifices is inferior to what they can produce in their imagination immediately at zero cost, in the comfort and security provided by the society they disdain. What would otherwise be a purely personal idiosyncrasy becomes socially ominous when it generates a whole vision of the world in which very real and often very painful predicaments are dealt with as if they were entirely different from what they are.

That vision is the vision of cosmic justice. In addition to its other dangers, the quest for cosmic justice is incompatible with the fundamental principles of the American revolution—the rule of law, individual freedom, and democratic government.

THE RULE OF LAW

Laws are not simply edicts backed by the power to enforce them. All societies proclaim duties and prohibitions which they are prepared to enforce, but not all societies have the rule of law. Neither the individual tyranny of a despot nor the collective tyranny of a totalitarian political party under communism or fascism represents the rule of law, even though there may be many individual laws under both forms of government. The rule of law—"a government of laws and not of men"—implies rules *known in advance*, applied generally, and constraining the rulers as well as the ruled. Freedom implies *exemptions* from the power of the rulers and a corresponding limitation on the scope of all laws, even those of democratically elected governments. "Congress shall make no law—" the First Amendment to the Constitution of the United States begins in spelling out some of the exemptions from laws which constitute the right to freedom. Democracy implies majority sanction as the basis for laws, but democracy by itself implies nothing about either freedom or the rule of law. A majority may destroy the freedom of a minority or make the issuance of edicts as arbitrary and discriminatory as it wishes. The systematic denial of rights to American blacks in the Southern states during the Jim Crow era was a classic example of democratic despotism.

Among the forces driving democratic governments toward an expansion of their powers beyond the point where these powers threaten freedom is that not only people of towering genius or towering presumptions, but also people of towering ambitions have a vested interest in such an expansion. As Alexis de Tocqueville put it: "It may easily be seen that almost all the able and ambitious members of a democratic community will labor unceasingly to extend the powers of government, because they all hope at some time or other to wield those powers themselves."[6] If nothing else, they can easily imagine themselves and others of similar disposition "running the country," with all the casual disregard of other people's individual freedom that this implies.

If general rules, known in advance, are at the heart of the rule of law, then such rules are inherently incompatible with cosmic justice. That inherent incompatibility shows itself in many ways, including issues involving equal treatment, property rights, burdens of proof, and the general role of judges in the carrying out of laws.

Equal Processes versus Equal Results

Rules equally applicable to all are not the same as rules with equal impact on all. Anatole France dramatized the distinction in his famous sarcastic remark: "The law, in its majestic equality, forbids the rich as well as the poor to sleep under bridges, to beg in the streets and to steal bread." In today's American legal doctrine, that is called "disparate impact." Many public and private acts and policies with disparate impacts on different segments of the population are banned as discriminatory, even when these acts and policies apply the same procedures and standards to everyone.[7] However, an understanding that equal rules do not mean equal consequences goes much farther back in history than the 1971 doctrine of disparate impact or Anatole France's remark in 1894. Nor was this understanding confined to the political left. In his scathing *Reflections on the Revolution in France*, Edmund Burke said, "all men have equal rights; but not to equal things."[8] James FitzJames Stephen pointed out in 1873 that every law and every moral rule, being general propositions, "must affect indiscriminately rather than equally."[9]

In short, the inherent conflict between equal rules and equal results has been recognized in theory for at least two centuries, even though many of our contemporaries proclaim, as if it were some new discovery or deeper insight of theirs, that laws that are "formally" equal may affect different groups differently. From this they conclude that "real" equality must supersede merely formal equality—which is to say that cosmic justice must trump traditional justice. A common expression of this view is that "equality before the law without economic, political, and social opportunities is a mockery."[10] What is crucial at this point is not whether we agree or disagree with one or the other of these conceptions but that we clearly understand that they are *mutually incompatible*, that their fundamental contradictions cannot be blended or finessed.

Much of the legal history of the past several decades has been a confused tangle of Supreme Court cases attempting to reconcile these irreconcilable principles, especially in cases involving affirmative action, which have produced many 5 to 4 decisions, cases decided in opposite ways by the same nine Supreme Court justices, and cases with no given majority for a particular decision, but only shifting majorities for particular sections of the decision. Too often this confusion has been made a virtue with claims that the "complexity" of the issues precluded a "simplistic" choice. But irreconcilability is not complexity. Nor are attempts to square the circle signs of deeper insight. More generally, there is also no *a priori* reason to prefer complex resolutions over simpler ones for, as Aristotle said, "things that are true and things that are better are almost always easier to believe in."[11] In short, the truth often seems "simplistic" by comparison with elaborate attempts to evade the truth.

The difference between the equal treatment of traditional justice and the equal results or equal prospects of cosmic justice affect many other kinds of issues. From the perspective of those who seek cosmic justice, freedom of speech does not mean simply exemption from government control of content but includes as well the *means* of making speech heard. In other words, it requires more government intervention, rather than less, so as to force some citizens to make available resources to enable other citizens to exercise their free speech rights.

Thus shopping malls, airports, and even private housing developments have been forced to relinquish their rights as property owners to keep trespassers out and instead are forced to allow people to pass out leaflets or solicit money on their property, in disregard of the desires of those who wish to use these malls, airports, or private housing developments for the purposes for which they were designed and built, without being disturbed or harassed. Those with the cosmic view of justice likewise favor forcing radio and television broadcasters to give, or to sell below the market rate, time for political messages or to broadcast what some third parties choose to define as "public service" programming.

Within the American system of constitutional government, a sharp distinction has been made traditionally between those actions forbidden to the government and those actions which private individuals or organizations may engage in. Within the framework of traditional justice, where constitutional rights are essentially exemptions from the power of the state, rights to equal treatment or to freedom of speech or religion apply where there is "state action" but not when only private individuals or organizations are involved. Thus, in principle, a private individual can evict from his home anyone who uses the word "broccoli" but it would be a violation of the constitutional right to free speech for the government to forbid the use of this word, either in general or even just within that same house.

We might regard the homeowner who ordered people out of his house for saying "broccoli" as being at best eccentric and certainly unreasonable, if not of questionable sanity. But the whole point of rights is that, within wide limits, those who exercise those rights do not have to satisfy others as to the wisdom or virtue of their decisions.

All this changes radically, however, within the framework of cosmic justice. If some group is not receiving justice, then whether this is due to governmental or private actions is seen as secondary, if it is relevant at all. Nowhere has this been more acutely felt than in issues involving racial discrimination. Here it is often insisted that everyone is entitled to equal treatment and also that "each group must advocate and insist upon its piece of the pie" and that there has been a "failure of the private sector to address the issue forthrightly."[12]

At this point, with our focus being on the general framework of law, rather than on the merits of particular legislation or policies, what matters most are not the merits or demerits of these particular legal issues and judicial decisions as social policy, but how all this affects the maintenance of the rule of law. Constitutional rights that are essentially exemptions from government power under traditional concepts of justice become reasons for the further extension of government power under cosmic concepts of justice. Cosmic justice cannot be achieved with "a government of laws and not of men" that simply establishes a legal framework within which individuals are free to make their own decisions and arrange their own voluntary transactions on whatever terms are mutually agreeable. For cosmic justice, someone must *oversee* the social results of these individual transactions and intervene directly to ensure that the desired social results or prospects are arranged.

Much focus on the desirability of the various outcomes being sought distracts attentions from the fundamental change of processes required to pursue those outcomes. Metaphors about how "society" should "arrange"[13] this or that result evade the institutional reality that someone must be empowered to constrict other people's freedom—and thus evade the need to weigh whether the expected value of the result being sought, given the chances of achieving it, is greater or less than the expected value of the loss of freedom that this effort entails.

Moreover, while traditional justice concerns rules of interaction between flesh-and-blood human beings, cosmic justice concerns abstract categories, whose prospects or results are to be adjusted to the taste of third parties. These abstractions reach across the generations and the collective claims that are made range from territorial irredentism to affirmative action and group reparations. Since the people involved in these inter-temporal abstractions are never all present as flesh-and-blood human beings at any given time, it is impossible for them to resolve their concerns by engaging in voluntary transactions, so that some superior power must, at some particular point in time, adjudicate their differences and impose a "solution."

The collectivization of otherwise individual decisions and the transfer of the power to make and enforce these collective decisions to some surrogate individual or institutions has further consequences. For example, these surrogate decision-makers are now morally accountable for the particular consequences of particular decisions, rather than being simply umpires responsible for maintaining a given framework of general rules. Unlike the cosmos, these decisions-makers can be blamed for preventable unhappiness.

Unfortunately, the inherent scarcity of resources means that all the evils that are preventable seriatim are not preventable simultaneously. Thus the apparent ability of "society" to prevent particular evils vastly exceeds its ability to actually prevent those same evils at the same time. One consequence of this is that there are now more reasons for various segments of society to fight each other politically, and perhaps physically, over benefits that were once shared peacefully and unconsciously through the ordinary operations of the marketplace.

The question is not simply whether the justice — however defined — of the outcome is better or worse under autonomous individual decision-making or collective surrogate decision-making. What must also be taken into account is the difference in the respective *costs* of achieving these different results, including both social strife and the loss of individual freedom. Moreover, the justice of the outcome cannot be independent of these costs, since "justice at all costs" is not justice. In addition, the concentration of political power creates dangers that the history of the twentieth century has all too tragically demonstrated.

There are many examples of the constraints imposed on the freedom of some in order to produce cosmic justice for others. More to the point, from the perspective of society as a whole, is the undermining of the rule of law in order to achieve particular results. For example, the Equal Employment Opportunity Commission has decreed that inequalities of employment opportunities growing out of mental illness are to be counterbalanced by government policy, so that employers are not permitted to "discriminate" against the mentally ill in hiring. Thus questions about prior incarceration in a mental hospital are not permitted during an employment interview under the E.E.O.C. guidelines and, once hired, mentally ill workers' special needs must be "reasonably" accommodated by the employer. For example, partitions may have to be put up around a worker with schizophrenia who is easily distracted, and even a lack of judgment in carrying out work duties may have to be allowed for in others. In short, the mentally ill are another group suffering disabilities "through no fault of their own" who are to be made whole at other people's expense—which can include personal or social disasters, as well as financial losses.

Preferential treatment is prescribed for the mentally ill in the name of equality—or an absence of "discrimination"—since it is *equalizing* treatment to counter-balance undeserved disadvantages. The term "cosmic justice" seems particularly more appropriate here than "social justice," since no claim is made that mental illness must be the result of social decisions or social conditions, though such disabilities are still unjust from the standpoint of the kind of cosmos we would prefer, if these matters were in our hands.

As already noted, one of the characteristics of the rule of law is that legal requirements be *known in advance.* Many laws, such as those dealing with vagrancy, have been invalidated by appellate courts as "void for vagueness," on grounds that what they require cannot be known to the citizen beforehand. Yet, increasingly, laws and policies seeking to achieve "social justice" or cosmic justice have been allowed to stand by the courts, even when there is no way for those subject to these laws to know in advance whether or not they have violated them. For example, the employer of a person with a history of mental illness or physical disability cannot know in advance whether what he has provided for that employee's special benefit constitutes "reasonable accommodation" to that illness or that disability. This knowledge can only come after the fact, when a court decides whether or not to award millions of dollars in damages to the employee and the employee's attorneys.

An employer cannot avoid a charge of racial discrimination merely by treating all employees and all job applicants the same, regardless of their race. "Disparate impact" statistics will help determine *after the fact* whether the employer's conduct is judged to be discriminatory toward minorities—or whether it represented "reverse discrimination" against some members of the majority population. Before the fact, there is often no way to know which way a court trial would turn out. In short, there is no rule of law. This is not a result of some deficiency in the way particular laws have been written or administered. It is inherent in the process of seeking cosmic justice, since general rules can produce only indiscriminate results, not equal results or results fitting some preconceived notion of "diversity."

Such loose expressions as "reasonably" accommodating those with disabilities are not mere verbal lapses. *There is no way to specify in precise general rules, known beforehand, what might be necessary to achieve results that would meet the standards of cosmic justice.* In short, there can be no rule of law for such things and courts seeking cosmic justice can no longer strike down such laws as "void for vagueness." These edicts do not happen to be vague, they are necessarily vague. They could not be otherwise. Thus "discrimination" cannot be left with a clear prospective meaning, such as applying different standards to members of different groups or subjecting some to more onerous processes than others. For purposes of cosmic justice, discrimination must be defined by retrospective results, whether "disparate impact" or "hostile environments" or a failure to provide "reasonable accommodation." This is only one of many ways in which the quest for cosmic justice is incompatible with the rule of law.

All too often, public outrage is focussed on particular policies, such as those of the E.E.O.C. regarding the hiring of the mentally ill, when in fact it is the more general erosion of the rule of law itself that is the real damage that is greater than the sum of all the particular damages created by all the particular policies and court decisions in which this erosion is embodied. A growing penumbra of uncertainty around laws in general makes courtrooms dangerous places for honest citizens and a threat that the dishonest can use for legalized extortion. Perhaps most insidious of all, loss of confidence in the law and the courts undermines civic morale and the cohesiveness of society in general.

In summary, cosmic justice attempts to create equal results or equal prospects, with little or no regard for whether the individuals or groups involved are in equal circumstances or have equal capabilities or equal personal drives. To do this, it cannot operate under general rules, the essence of law, but must create categories of people entitled to various outcomes, regardless of their own inputs. Moreover, it often does this *sub rosa*, by creating huge burdens of proof for any criteria that reveal the inequalities of capabilities and circumstances, while assuming with little or no evidence that only malign intentions or systemic bias could explain unequal results. "Affirmative action" is perhaps the classic example of this approach but it is only one example.

If equality looks radically different from the perspective of cosmic justice, so does bias. Traditional standards of admissions to colleges and universities, for example, have been characterized as "admissions systems that favored the white and the wealthy."[14] It is no doubt true that white and wealthy individuals can meet high academic standards a higher percentage of the time than those who are neither. But it says nothing about the validity of these standards as predictors of later academic or other achievements that those with advantages met the criteria more often than those without them.

Foreign examples in which we have no vested interest or ideological predisposition may illustrate the point even better. It has, for example, been claimed that the Chinese minority in colonial Malaya was favored by the policies of the British rulers there because the Chinese prospered more so than the Malays under those policies and Chinese children went on to higher education more often than Malay children did. Indeed, even after colonial Malaya became the independent nation of Malaysia, the Chinese continued for some time to have double the incomes of the Malays and Chinese students outnumbered Malay students at the University of Malaysia. Yet it was also true that the British colonial government provided free education for the Malays, while the Chinese had to pay to have their own children educated and the independent Malay government provided scholarships for the Malay children that were not equally available to the Chinese.[15] In both the colonial era and in the era of independence, Malays had rights that the Chinese did not have. By traditional concepts of prospective circumstances, it was the Malays who were favored under both regimes but, in cosmic terms, it was the Chinese. Again, what is crucial is not which perspective one chooses, but a clear understanding that they are inherently irreconcilable concepts that should not be confused with one another simply because they use the same words, for the actual senses of those same words are diametrically opposed.

From a cosmic perspective, in whatever circumstances A does better than B, those circumstances can be said to be circumstances "favoring" A. Note that there cannot be any such thing as *overcoming disadvantages* in this formulation. If businesses set up by poor Lebanese immigrants in colonial West Africa did better in competition with businesses set up there by more prosperous Europeans, then by cosmic definition that was because of Lebanese "advantages"—which consisted in this case of their being willing to work harder and longer hours, charging lower prices, accepting lower profits and a lower standard of living, and putting more efforts into understanding their African customers.[16] In short, *performance* differences between groups vanish into thin air by being subsumed under the concept of "advantages" or favorably biased prospects, even when the same prospects were available to both groups but only one group made the choices or the sacrifices, or had the capabilities, to make use of these prospects.

In their seeming simplicity, concepts of "advantage" and "disadvantage" can be treacherously misleading. While some advantages are simply differential benefits to one individual or group at the expense of some other individual or group—a zero-sum game—other things that are called "advantages" are in fact net benefits to the whole society that are unequally available to the various members of that society. The advantages of a nobleman over a peasant consist precisely in the peasant's obligations to give the nobleman a portion of his produce and his labor, as well as obedience and deference. In short, the peasant's losses are the nobleman's gains—a zero-sum game. However, when some people have far greater knowledge and facility in the design and production of computers than others, those others may nevertheless benefit greatly by the availability of computers suitably pre-programmed to be usable by millions of people who lack any real expertise. In this second case, society as a whole is better off, though to unequal degrees, because of the "advantages" possessed by those with a deeper knowledge of the operation of computers. By the same token, society as a whole can lose when attempts to eliminate these kinds of "advantages" eliminate benefits to millions who lack the advantages in question.

With a cosmic concept of bias or advantage, people seeking or justifying preferential policies often speak of such policies as being necessary to create "a level playing field." However, this phrase has a wholly different meaning outside the framework of cosmic justice. In traditional terms, what preferential policies create is a playing field tilting in favor of those whose performance on a level playing field would be inadequate. The point here is not to assess the particular merits of particular preferential policies or of preferential policies in general—which has been done elsewhere[17]—but to demonstrate the diametrically opposite meaning of the same phrase when used inside and outside the framework of cosmic justice.

Property Rights

Among the first rights to be sacrificed in the quest for cosmic justice are property rights. Clearly the owners of substantial property are very eligible candidates for the role of people enjoying privileged positions and therefore very eligible to have their legal rights sacrificed for the greater good of less fortunate people. However, this way of looking at things completely misconceives the role of property rights and of rights in general. Just as freedom of the press does not exist for the sake of that tiny minority of the population who are journalists, so property rights do not exist for the sake of those people with substantial property holdings. Both rights exist to serve social purposes reaching far beyond those who actually exercise these rights.

The whole operation of a democratic political system, and the kind of freedom it is intended to safeguard, would be undermined or destroyed if political power-holders could forbid journalists from saying things that were politically embarrassing by censoring the press "in the national interest" or by some other rationale. Such a power would be a blank check for violating all the other rights guaranteed by the Constitution to the population at large, for those violations could all be covered up if the press were controlled by politicians. In short, the principal beneficiaries of the right of freedom of the press are people who are not part of the press.

A free-market economy is as much dependent on property rights as the political system is on free speech rights. For a nation's investments to flow to those uses most highly valued by the consuming public, those who own assets must be free to deploy those assets where they can get the highest return. For huge undertakings, such as building a railroad system or creating factories that will manufacture millions of automobiles, individuals must be allowed to accumulate vast aggregations of wealth—whether their own or those of stockholders. For maximum incentives to make the best judgment of where investments should go, as well as maximum incentives to manage those investments in such as way as to maximize the chances of success, people must be free of limits on how much they are allowed to accumulate, even if others proclaim that they have "obscene" amounts of wealth.

The easiest way to see the effects of property rights is to see what happens in their absence or curtailment. Government abolition of private property in agricultural land has created food shortages in countries around the world, among people of every race, and in political systems of many sorts—even in countries that were once exporters of food from Eastern Europe or sub-Saharan Africa. Malnutrition and starvation were the price of collectivization of agriculture in the Soviet Union under Stalin and, in later years, only massive imports of food from the West prevented a repetition of the same dire experience. Yet the Soviet Union and Eastern Europe in general contained some of the most fertile land in the world and historically this region exported vast amounts of grain to Western Europe and elsewhere—before property rights in land were abolished. Moreover, the small plots of land that the Soviet government allowed individuals to cultivate on their own produced an entirely disproportionate amount of the agricultural output of the country—again showing the value of private property in output, even when the land was not privately owned. Nor was this unique as a dramatic demonstration of the difference between what people will produce for the benefit of themselves and their families, as compared to what they will produce when their rewards are constrained in the name of some larger collectivity.

Mere curtailment of property rights has often produced serious economic problems. Even when property is allowed to remain in private hands, but the price charged by property owners is restricted by law, detrimental effects on output, product quality, and availability have been common around the world and over thousands of years of history.[18] Food has in many places and in various periods of history been a special target of price controls, often on the plausible-sounding ground that food is so basic a need that the poor must be assured access to it at a price that they can afford. Yet, all too often, mass hunger has followed in the wake of price controls on food, whether during the era of the French revolution, in modern African nations, or in Asia. Similarly, housing shortages have followed rent control, whether in New York City, Paris, Hong Kong, Melbourne, Stockholm, or other places around the world.[19] Price controls on medical treatment have led to long waiting lines in doctors' offices and long waiting lists for operations, whether in China, Europe, or elsewhere.[20]

The inefficiency of political control of an economy has been demonstrated more often, in more places, and under more varied conditions, than almost anything outside the realm of pure science. Put differently, property rights and the associated rights of free contract in a free market have a major impact on the economic well-being of masses of people, far beyond those relatively few who own substantial property or who are in a position to hire others or engage in major economic transactions. The property rights guaranteed to the few are essential to the economic well-being of the many, just as the freedom of the press is not just a special-interest benefit to journalists. Yet property rights are often treated as if they were in fact only special-interest benefits for the more fortunate and therefore rights to be sacrificed in pursuit of cosmic justice for others.

From the standpoint of the rule of law, none of this needs to be argued. For Americans, at least, the matter was settled long ago when the Constitution of the United States declared that no person could be "deprived of life, liberty, or property, without due process of law, nor shall private property be taken for public use without just compensation." By the second half of the twentieth century, however, all of this was being eroded rapidly by judges. Moreover, this erosion and undermining of property rights was applauded in the leading law schools and by the intelligentsia in general.

Professor Laurence Tribe of the Harvard Law School, for example, sees the constitution's "built-in bias against redistribution of wealth" as a benefit to "entrenched wealth."[21] That is, he sees it as simply a benefit to special interests, in a way in which he would not regard freedom of the press as just a special-interest benefit to journalists. Note also how the term "bias" is used here in a sense parallel with the usage of those who say that the Chinese have been "favored" over the Malays. When the rule of law is seen as a bias, cosmic justice has been quietly enshrined and the principles of the American constitution quietly repealed.

Judicial Activism
The role of judges is of course crucial in the law—and especially to maintaining the rule of law, as distinguished from a system of arbitrary edicts from those who hold power. Here again, the tra-

ditional concept of justice leads to a wholly different role for judges than their role as seen by those pursuing the quest for cosmic justice.

The traditional conception of the role of judges was expressed thousands of years ago by Aristotle, who said that a judge should "be allowed to decide as few things as possible." His discretion should be limited to "such points as the lawgiver has not already defined for him." Moreover, the law itself must be an application of rules to be used for the guidance of others besides the litigants, for its decisions are "not particular but prospective and general."[22] By contrast, *New York Times* columnist and legal writer Anthony Lewis praised Supreme Court Justice Harry Blackmun because Blackmun "focused the most on the actual people whose lives were touched by the cases"[23]—in other words, the litigants before him and perhaps a similarly circumstanced segment of the society. But those affected by Supreme Court decisions include all those who are affected by the stability, reliability, and just application of laws—and that means everyone in the whole society, not just the litigants or those like the litigants. If the claim is implied that Blackmun took account of all the ramifications of his decisions on all others affected beyond the courtroom, then this is claiming what no judge or any other human being can ever do.

A judge cannot "do justice" directly in the cases before him. This view was strongly expressed in a small episode in the life of Justice Oliver Wendell Holmes. After having lunch with Judge Learned Hand, Holmes entered his carriage to be driven away. As he left, Judge Hand's parting salute was:

"Do justice, sir, do justice."

Holmes ordered the carriage stopped.

"That is not my job," Holmes said to Judge Hand. "It is my job to apply the law."[24]

Elsewhere, Holmes wrote that his primary responsibility as a judge was "to see that the game is played according to the rules whether I like them or not."[25] In one of his U.S. Supreme Court decisions, Holmes said: "When we know what the source of the law has said that it shall be, our authority is at an end."[26] Another Supreme Court opinion by Holmes ended: "I am not at liberty to consider the justice of the Act."[27]

The case for upholding legal principles, known and relied upon by others, is precisely that *it can be done,* and done while preserving a free society, whereas playing cases by ear requires far more knowledge than anyone possesses and is incompatible with the rule of law and the freedom which depends on that rule. The specific virtues of particular laws or particular judicial interpretations of laws—their justice, compassion, equality, or adjustment to social realities, for example—are of course important. But a major part of the benefits of law comes from its being law as such, from its being a dependable framework within which millions of people may plan and act, whether or not the particular laws have other specific virtues. Thus Christians and Jews were able to prosper in business under the dependable laws of the Ottoman Empire, even though these laws denied them equality and made them subordinate in many ways to Moslems. Ironically, economists have been discovering the enormous importance of the rule of law at about the same time as judges have been sacrificing the rule of law to attempts to make the law more just, compassionate, equal, or more in tune with the judges' own perceptions of social realities.

The role of such concerns as justice and compassion are very different in legislation than in the later judicial interpretation of legislation. When Oliver Wendell Holmes said "I hate justice" as a judicial consideration,[28] he was not saying that justice did not belong in the law. He was saying that it was not the judge's function to put it there, that this was a legislative function. Much the same view was later echoed by Judge Robert H. Bork, when he said, "justice is for the Congress and the President to administer, if they see fit, through the creation of new law."[29] It might seem that, if justice is something desirable in the law, then the question of who puts it there is secondary, if not trivial. On the contrary, however, the separation of roles in creating law is crucial to the preservation of the rule of law itself.

Legislative enactments, presidential actions, and amendments to the Constitution are all things which publicly announce changes in the law of the land, providing foreknowledge of changes in the legal framework within which free people may act and plan. Moreover, all these processes are ultimately responsible to the people themselves and can be reversed if the people find them onerous. Judge-made innovations are, in effect, ex post facto laws, which are expressly forbidden by the Constitution and abhorrent to the very concept of the rule of law. For the courts to strike like a bolt from the blue hitting an unsuspecting citizen, who was disobeying no law that he could have known about beforehand, is the essence of judicial tyranny, however moral or just the judges may imagine their innovation to be. The harm is not limited to the particular damage this may do in the particular case, great as this may sometimes be, but makes all other laws into murky storm clouds, potential sources of other bolts from the blue, contrary to the whole notion of "a government of laws and not of men."

The difference between cosmic justice and traditional justice means a huge difference in the power of judges. Under cosmic justice, the judge's role is to decide whether the behavior of each of the parties fits the judge's notions of what they should have done. Under traditional justice, the judge decides the much narrower question as to what each party had a right to do, at that party's own discretion, under existing laws and agreements. Cosmic justice not only makes judges roving second-guessers but surrounds prospective agreements with a penumbra of uncertainty, making such agreements harder to reach and carry out.

The quest for cosmic justice via the judiciary—law as an "agent of change," as it is often phrased—quietly repeals one of the foundations of the American revolution. It reduces a free people to a subject people, subject now to the edicts of unelected judges enforcing "evolving standards" and made more heedless by their exalted sense of moral superiority. It is one of the most dangerous of the many ways in which towering presumptions are a threat to the freedom of Americans.

Burdens of Proof

No aspect of traditional justice is more fundamental than the presumption of innocence in criminal cases and the corresponding burden of proof on plaintiffs, rather than on accused respondents, in civil cases. Otherwise, the ability of government to throw people in jail, or to ruin them financially, because of its own vast powers and resources that can be put behind any trumped-up charges, would render all other freedoms meaningless. Whatever the high-sounding ideals of the law or the proclamations of freedom in the Constitution, the operative principle would be: Anger the power-holders and you will be destroyed. No principle could be more diametrically opposed to the whole meaning of the American revolution. Yet that is the direction in which American law has been evolving, at an accelerating pace, during the twentieth century.

The first field in which the burden of proof began to shift to the defendant or respondent was anti-trust law. The most sweeping and dramatic shift was in civil rights law, which was followed by similar developments in environmental laws, tort liability, sexual harassment policies, and laws and policies applied to families. In all these areas, what was being sought was cosmic justice for some, with the usual disregard of the costs of this for others. These others include not only the particular losers, or classes of losers, in legal cases. It includes everyone in the society, for all are jeopardized by the ease with which burdens of proof can be shifted to the accused—which means not simply existing classes of criminal defendants or respondents in civil cases, but whatever additional classes may be created in future, based on a succession of legal precedents that have quietly repealed one of the basic principles of American constitutional law.

Dangerous as such powers are in the hands of government officials, these officials are not the only group of people who are allowed to impose high costs on others at low costs to themselves. While government officials can directly spend the taxpayers' money to finance the pursuit of their charges against others, a private attorney may also collect millions of dollars in attorney's fees from the taxpayers for what is called "pro bono" work—meaning that his client doesn't pay—in the increasingly wide range of cases involving "civil rights." While this term historically referred to cases of discrimination against minorities, it has expanded far beyond that meaning to include, for example, the eviction of tenants (of any race) from federally subsidized housing for their own misconduct. The most blond-haired and blue-eyed alcoholic or pyromaniac can sue under these "civil rights" laws for being deprived of a taxpayer-provided benefit and his attorney, if successful, can collect far more from the taxpayers than the client collects, all the while being considered to be engaged in work *pro bono publica*—for the benefit of the public— as if he were a selfless volunteer.

The driving purpose of such legal developments has not been a desire to subvert the Constitution. Typically, it has been to pursue some aspect of cosmic justice. From this perspective, the subversion of the Constitution is an incidental by-product. Moreover, for each particular piece of legislation or any given legal case, the incremental damage done to the Constitution may seem to be slight. It is only in the aggregate that this pursuit of cosmic justice "at all costs" becomes a dangerous destruction of the rights that define and defend a free society.

Those subject to the destruction of their rights—and hence the jeopardizing of others' rights through legal precedent— have typically been some group easily demonized within the context of a vision of cosmic justice. Big business has historically been a prime target, long before those accused of being racists, environmental polluters, child abusers, and other defendants who have become featured targets more recently. The Sherman Antitrust Act of 1890 forbad "monopolization"—a term undefined except *ex post* in litigation—and the later

Clayton Act of 1914 and Robinson-Patman Act of 1936 were at least equally vague.

In these latter statutes, various acts committed by businesses are illegal when they "substantially lessen competition" in any line of commerce. When the courts have deemed the acts of a small rubber stamp manufacturer with only 19 employees, and with 70 competitors in the same city, to have met the criterion of substantially lessening competition,[30] the ability of any business to know in advance whether what it is doing will be considered to fall under the Clayton or Robinson-Patman Acts is questionable at best, if not wholly illusory.

More fundamental than the vagueness of these acts is the shift of the burden of proof to the accused. The government or a private plaintiff need only make a *prima facie* case—that is, a case that does not even have to meet the standard of a "preponderance of evidence," much less "beyond a reasonable doubt," to force the accused to prove his innocence. In many cases, the elusiveness of the concepts and the inconclusiveness of the evidence make it impossible for anybody on either side to prove anything. *The accused lose those cases.* Thus the rubber stamp manufacturer with only 19 people working for him "did not prove affirmatively" that his giving discounts to some customers "did not lessen competition or tend to prevent it," according to the Court of Appeals.[31]

While this particular case provided a precedent only for the Second Circuit Court of Appeals, many other cases have likewise been lost by the accused because they could not disprove *prima facie* cases consisting solely of the fact that they gave some customers discounts. When the Borden Company sold evaporated milk to jobbers who bought in large quantity at a discount below what it charged grocery stores, or when Standard Oil sold gasoline at a discount to jobbers who likewise bought in large quantities, both the companies lost their cases because they could not conclusively prove their innocence under the law.[32]

Many anti-trust cases, especially those involving the Robinson-Patman Act, show a pattern that would later appear in the very different realm of affirmative action cases — reversals and re-reversals as the cases go up the chain of appeals, climaxed by 5 to 4 decisions in the Supreme Court. While those with a self-congratulatory bent could attribute this to the "complexity" of the issues and to their unwillingness to be "simplistic," more fundamentally the problem is not complexity but contradiction — between statutory attempts to produce cosmic justice and the underlying principles of the Constitution, which are necessarily violated in these attempts.

COSMIC JUSTICE VERSUS DEMOCRATIC FREEDOM

Definitions

Democracy can be defined in a very straightforward way: majority rule. There are, of course, many variations of majority rule, ranging from town-meeting democracy to the representative democracy of legislatures. Moreover, even majority rule may be constrained, as it is in the United States, within constitutional limits that can be changed only by a super-majority in Congress, combined with a super-majority of the state legislatures. But the core idea is clear enough, even though some confusion has been introduced in our times by trying to include within the very def-

175

inition of democracy various end-results expected or desired, such as freedom, the dignity of the individual, and other goals. But democratic government is democratic government, whether its decisions are wise or foolish, humane or vicious.

Freedom, however, has long been defined in radically different ways by those with different visions—and especially by those in quest of cosmic justice. The traditional conception of freedom as *exemptions from power* has already been illustrated by such language in the Constitution's Bill of Rights as "Congress shall make no law . . ." Note that the possible merits of these laws is not at issue. When it comes to freedom of religion, or of the press, for example, Congress shall make *no* law. Exemptions from any laws that Congress might want to make is, in effect, the definition of these freedoms. By implication, *power is the ability to restrict people's options* and freedom is an exemption from having one's options restricted in such matters as religion or the expression of ideas.

All this changes, however, within the framework of cosmic justice, where freedom and power are conceived in entirely different terms. Among the many expressions of this very different view is that in R. H. Tawney's *Equality*:

> Power may be defined as the capacity of an individual, or group of individuals, to modify the conduct of other individuals or groups in the manner which he desires, and to prevent his own conduct from being modified in the manner in which he does not.[33]

Innocuous as this definition might seem, it implies a radical departure from the traditional conception of freedom as embodied in constitutional exemptions from government power. The much broader notion of modifying other people's behavior includes power in the traditional sense but is by no means limited to it. For example, when an athlete is offered a multimillion-dollar contract to play football, that may well modify any previous plans he had to become a dentist or an accountant. Few people would regard that as a restriction of his pre-existing options. On the contrary, it is adding an option that may prove to be far more attractive, though the athlete remains free to make any of the other choices that were available to him before. From these very different conceptions of freedom and power flow very different practical conclusions about political and economic issues. In traditional terms, he has lost no freedom to those with power. In cosmic terms, exemplified by Tawney's definition, he has.

From the cosmic conception of power flows the otherwise anomalous notion of "economic power" that has exercised an influence ranging from anti-trust policy to apologetics for communism. A "concentration of economic power," as Tawney phrased it,[34] serves as a justification for government restrictions on those businesses which attract a large proportion of the consumers of a given product. Thus a firm whose product is bought by two-thirds of the consumers of such products is said to "control" two-thirds of that market and of course to have "economic power" that government must contain or neutralize in some way.

In the absence of the notion of "economic power" and such accompanying rhetoric as "control," this situation is more likely to be seen as one in which two-thirds of the consumers prefer a given firm's product over similar products made by competitors—a situation far from ominous and perhaps one in which congratulations are in order for the firm that did such a better job of providing what the consumers wanted. But, of course, this more sanguine way of looking at things would not justify an expansion of government power to offset "economic power." Such expansions of government power have included not only anti-trust laws and other regulations of businesses but have extended all the way to socialism and communism. Whatever the specific merits or demerits of any of these policies and institutional changes in themselves, the concept of "economic power" allows concerns about expansions of government power to be finessed by saying that this is not a net increase of power or a net diminution of freedom, since it merely offsets private "economic power," in order to protect the public.

For the sake of following a particular example of the application of the concept of "economic power," we may again look to Tawney, though he was in no sense unique or even unusual among those seeking cosmic justice. According to Tawney, "84 percent of the output" in the British coal industry of his time was "produced by 323 concerns employing over 1,000 workers each, and nearly one-fifth was produced by 57 firms"—all of this representing "a concentration of economic control."[35] Similar statistics have been cited for innumerable industries in many countries, as if such retrospective statistics are proof of prospective "control" of anything. Indeed, in any line of human endeavor, some x number of producers produce two-thirds, three-quarters, or whatever other percentage one chooses, of the total output.

For example, in the same year in which Tawney's book was published (1931) just 13 baseball players hit more than half the home runs in the American League, even though there were about two hundred players in the league. The same was true in the year for which coal concentration statistics were cited (1923).[36] Nothing has been more common, in countries around the world and over centuries of history, than for a fraction of the participants in any given activity to produce a disproportionate amount of that activity.[37] Yet nothing has been more common among intellectuals than to regard such disproportionalities as unusual, if not sinister.

The relevance of all this here is that the cosmic perspective on the world which leads to such notions as "economic power" and "control" provides a rationale for an expansion of government power that does indeed reduce pre-existing options and thus constrict freedom.

Buying and Selling Freedom

Among the American constitutional barriers to the expansion of federal government power is the Tenth Amendment:

> The powers not delegated to the United States by the Constitution, nor prohibited by it to the States, are reserved to the States respectively, or to the people.

In other words, the federal government may do only what it is specifically authorized to do, while the people or the individual states may do whatever they are not specifically forbidden to do. This barrier against the centralization of power is one of the fundamental protections of freedom and epitomizes the spirit of the American revolution. In the absolute monarchies of old or the dictatorships of the twentieth century, all power flowed from the center, with regional or local governments being simply subordinate units of the central government, rather than autonomous authorities with their own areas of exemption from the power of the national state. This deliberate splitting up of a country's political power by the Constitution has been one of the bulwarks of individual freedom and democratic self-government. Unfortunately, no constitutional provision has been more consistently eroded or more blatantly ignored in the latter half of the twentieth century than the Tenth Amendment.

Partly this has been done by judicial sleight of hand since the days of the New Deal and then, especially since the 1960s, by the federal government's attaching conditions to its ever-expanding largesse to states and to private institutions—conditions which the national government has no constitutional authority to impose directly by law, but which they impose indirectly by the threat to cut off billions of dollars of subsidies on which these states and institutions now depend. In short, the federal government has been buying up the freedom of the people with the people's own tax money.

For the judiciary, vast expansions of the scope of federal power during the heady crusades of the New Deal—many of them fueled by notions of cosmic justice—were justified by the constitutional provision that Congress had the right to regulate "interstate commerce." This provision became a blank check by which virtually anything that Congress wanted to regulate was simply called "interstate commerce." In a landmark case involving federal regulation of agriculture, the Supreme Court ruled that a man who grew his own food in his own back yard was engaged in interstate commerce and thus was subject to federal control. For decades, vast expansions of federal power were repeatedly and almost automatically rationalized as authorized by Congress' power to regulate interstate commerce.

So deeply ingrained was this new tradition that there was consternation when, in 1995, the Supreme Court ruled that carrying a gun near a school was *not* interstate commerce.[38] The justices split 5 to 4 and most editorial comment centered on whether it was desirable to allow people to carry guns near schools, not on the nature of constitutional government. The fact that most states already banned the carrying of guns in or around schools, and that all states had the authority to do so, meant that the real issue was not the safety of children but the scope of federal power. Unfortunately, the scope of federal power was no longer an issue for many Americans, since the Tenth Amendment had quietly been repealed by judicial erosion, so this first setback in decades for the blank-check interpretation of the interstate commerce clause caught many people by surprise. Moreover, the fact that this was a 5 to 4 decision meant that it might turn out to be nothing more than an isolated blip on the screen of history, rather than the beginning of a restoration of the constitutional principle of limited national government power.

Since the 1960s, federal government power over states, private institutions, and individuals, has expanded far faster than the pace made possible by the accretions growing out of particular Supreme Court cases. Crucial to this whole development has been a vast expansion of federal "aid" to innumerable activities from highway building to university research and from urban redevelopment to hospitals and adoption agencies. With this aid have come conditions—typically modest conditions at first and then, over the years, increasingly detailed, restrictive,

and arbitrary regulations. Thus the federal government can pre-
scribe the color that fire extinguishers must be painted in state
or private buildings or whether private child-care facilities must
hire people with communicable diseases or mental illness.
Although such sweeping powers come from buying up people's
freedom, often there is little alternative but to sell, since there is
no realistic way for most individuals or institutions to refuse to
sell their freedom and return to the status quo ante.

If the federal government pours hundreds of millions of dollars in research grants and student subsidies into Harvard, then
Yale cannot reject the same subsidies without falling decisively
behind Harvard in all the areas in which they compete for students, faculty, and academic standing. There is no way for Yale
to restore the status quo ante unilaterally. In virtually every activity in which there is competition—which is to say, in virtually
every activity—no given recipient of federal largesse can refuse
to sell local autonomy or institutional freedom without losing
out to other institutions that were comparable before the expansion of federal largesse.

No institution has been more traditionally one of local control than the public schools. Yet the growing scope of federal
subsidy and control, particularly through the Department of
Education, has successively removed more and more decisions
from the parents and voters in local school districts, transferring
those decisions to Washington. It simply does not matter
whether parents, voters, or local officials are up in arms against
"whole language" methods of teaching reading or the promotion
of avant-garde sexual attitudes in schools, if these ideas are in
vogue among those in Washington who control the purse
strings. It does not matter if Hispanic parents want their children

to be taught in the English language if federal bureaucrats favor so-called bilingual programs in which most courses are taught in Spanish. It does not matter if local schools want to maintain tighter discipline if federal guidelines make it impossible to run a tight ship.

Despite numerous studies showing that the amount of money spent per pupil has little or no effect on the quality of education, federal officials are constantly pushing for an expansion of federal aid to education under the guise of "investing" in our children's futures. However little effect this money will have on the quality of these children's education, it has had an enormous effect on the expansion of federal power. This money may not buy a better education for the students but it unquestionably buys up the freedom of parents, voters, and local authorities, and transfers decision-making power to Washington.

Nor are schools at all unique in this respect. It does not matter if a hospital does not want a pharmacist with AIDS handling medicines to be administered to its patients if the institution will lose millions of dollars in federal money for transferring him to some other activity where his disease would be less dangerous. It does not matter if a child-care center does not want to hire someone with a history of mental illness to take care of its children if the federal government can cancel its subsidy for violating its "guidelines" for hiring the mentally ill. It does not matter what private physicians and their patients might want to do in treating a particular illness—even if these patients pay for treatment out of their own pockets—if those physicians treat other patients whose bills are paid by Medicare and thus falls under federal controls that apply to his practice in general.

Schemes to extend federal power into the nooks and crannies of local and even private activities are never publicly advertised as expansions of federal power, much less erosions of the Tenth Amendment, but always in terms of the wonderful goals they are said to achieve—"universal health care," "investing in our children's futures," "insuring a level playing field for all," etc. As many have warned in the past, freedom is unlikely to be lost all at once and openly. It is far more likely to be eroded away, bit by bit, amid glittering promises and expressions of noble ideals. Thus hard-earned freedoms for which many have fought and died have now been bought and sold for words or money, or both.

SUMMARY AND CONCLUSIONS

The government produced by the American revolution was unique, not only by contrast with the monarchies and other despotisms of its time, but also by contrast with other revolutions of its own and later eras. The French revolution of the succeeding decade used similar rhetoric, and was supported by such prominent figures in the American revolution as Thomas Jefferson and Thomas Paine, but nevertheless the French revolution was grounded on entirely different assumptions and of course took a different path all too characteristic of later revolutions that began with lofty ideals and ended with new and more ruthless despotism.

Where the American and the French revolutions differed most fundamentally was in the rule of law. Certain members of the French national assembly were deputized to go around the country as "representatives on mission" righting wrongs as they saw them, even when that required over-riding local organs of government or the laws they had created, or dismissing from office those whom these representatives found wanting. Representatives on mission even carried their own guillotine with them, to dispense their own brand of justice on the spot. At the national level as well, the "Committee of Public Safety" under Robespierre ruled by decrees that could over-ride any laws.

Limited powers and the supremacy of laws were at the heart of the Constitution established by the American revolution. Constitutional checks and balance and procedural safeguards were baffling to an ideological supporter of the French revolution like Condorcet, who saw such things as mere impediments to doing what was right and changing whatever needed changing. Much of what has been done in the United States— in the courts, in politics, and in the streets—in the latter half of the twentieth century is based on assumptions much more similar to those of the French revolution than of the American revolution.

When Chief Justice Earl Warren interrupted lawyers presenting legal arguments before the Supreme Court to ask "But is it right? Is it good?" he was much more in the tradition of the representatives on mission than in the tradition of "a government of laws and not of men." The many other judges at all levels who followed Warren's example—running school systems, changing voting laws, or even ordering legislatures to raise taxes to finance judicial ventures in social engineering—were likewise acting as representatives on mission, rather than preservers of a framework of law.

The Constitution of the United States is not a convoluted treatise or a collection of arcane concepts that only a priesthood of the bench or the law schools can decipher. Its crucial terms, such as "free speech" or "due process," already had historical meanings in English law before the American constitution was written by transplanted Englishmen. The much-vaunted "complexity" of constitutional law comes in most cases not from the Constitution itself but from clever attempts to evade the limits on government power set by the Constitution. The virtually unlimited judicial expansion of the concept of "interstate commerce" until it cancels many of those limits and nullifies the Tenth Amendment is perhaps the classic example.

The ideal of impartiality in the law, exemplified by statues of Justice blindfolded, implies that particular results for particular individuals and groups are to be disregarded when dispensing justice. It is precisely this conception of justice—at the heart of the American revolution—that is being disregarded. As was aptly said:

> The blindfolded Goddess of Justice has been encouraged to peek and she now says, with the jurists of the ancient regime, "First tell me who you are and then I'll tell you what your rights are."[39]

In politics, the great *non sequitur* of our time is that (1) things are not right and that (2) the government should make them right. Where right all too often means cosmic justice, trying to set things right means writing a blank check for a never-ending expansion of government power. That in turn means the quiet and piecemeal repeal of the American revolution and the freedom that it signified as an ideal for everyone. It means muffling the shot heard round the world and bringing back the old idea that some are booted and spurred to ride others. That they are riding with a heady sense of moral mission and personal gratification only makes them more dangerous.

Such moral and intellectual arrogance is in fundamental and irreconcilable conflict with the American creed of the common man. Someone once referred to the masses of immigrants coming to the United States as "the beaten men of beaten races." In one sense, he was right but, in a deeper sense, history has proved him profoundly wrong. From its colonial beginnings, American society was a "decapitated" society—largely lacking the topmost social layers of European society. The highest elites and the titled aristocracies had little reason to risk their lives crossing the Atlantic and then face the perils of pioneering. Most of the white population of colonial America arrived as indentured servants and the black population as slaves. Later waves of immigrants were disproportionately peasants and proletarians, even when they came from Western Europe, while those from the much-conquered regions of Eastern Europe and the Balkans clearly fit the descriptions of "beaten men from beaten races." The rise of American society to pre-eminence as an economic, political, and military power in the world was thus the triumph of the common man and a slap across the face to the presumptions of the arrogant, whether an elite of blood or books.

Now that the United States has its own large and growing class of presumptuously self-anointed moral exemplars—people who consider themselves "the conscience" of others—such people are as much in collision with the American creed of the common man as were those who once spoke of "the beaten men of beaten races." The disdain of these new elites for "Joe Sixpack" all too easily shades off into a sense of a need to deprive such lesser people of misused autonomy and "correcting" a system that allows the desires of ordinary people to prevail in the marketplace and in the social and political life of the country. Frontal assaults on basic American values would be suicidal, but that does not prevent piecemeal attacks or using other countries with very different values and different systems of government as models to be emulated.

Plain facts are easily forgotten and their crucial implications ignored when the whole orientation is toward finding fault with one's own country and seeking to "learn" from others. What that means too often in practice is that one focusses only on the flaws at home and only on the virtues—or assumed virtues— abroad. Thus Americans may fail to ask why America is one of a relative handful of rare exceptions among the countries of the world in having freedom, prosperity, military security, and social generosity. All these things may be of-coursed aside and the prerequisites for such benefits overlooked. For foreign countries, claimed virtues are all too readily accepted as realized virtues, whether these be "social justice" in Communist countries or spirituality in India.

It simply does not matter how many brides are beaten or even killed in India because their dowries are disappointing, nor does the continued oppression of the untouchables or the lethal mob violence erupting among various social groups in the country make a dent on the image of India as a land that has transcended the materialism and violence of the United States. Even pictures of Indians dancing in the streets after India exploded its first nuclear bomb did not disturb this vision, though Americans have never danced in the streets over their nuclear weapons. During the era of the ascendancy of communism, many American and other Western intellectuals remained unshakably sympathetic to the great social experiment going on in the Soviet Union, and many were positively gushing over Stalin, Mao, Castro, or other dictators whose people were fleeing en masse at the risk of their lives.

The net result of such attitudes is not simply that credit and discredit may be displaced. What is far more important—and more dangerous—is that there is little sense of the institutions and traditions which produce the enormous social and economic good fortune of Americans—and therefore little or no sense of the dangers from letting those institutions and traditions erode or be pushed aside for the sake of some political goal of the moment. Much of the world today and down through centuries of history has suffered the terrible consequences of unbridled government power, the prime evil that the writers of the American Constitution sought to guard against. Judges who "interpret" constitutional safeguards out of existence for the sake of some ideological crusade, presidents who over-reach their authority for personal or political reasons, and a Congress whose powers are extended into matters that the Constitution never empowered them to legislate about are all part of the quiet repeal of the American revolution.

Notes

The Quest for Cosmic Justice

1. Milton and Rose Friedman, *Free to Choose* (New York: Harcourt Brace Jovanovich, 1980), p. 146.

2. Adam Smith, *The Theory of Moral Sentiments* (Indianapolis: Liberty Classics, 1976), pp. 115, 120, 355.

3. Friedrich A. Hayek, *Law, Legislation and Liberty*, Vol. 2: *The Mirage of Social Justice* (Chicago: University of Chicago Press, 1978), pp. 33, 64.

4. Ibid., Vol. 1: *Rules and Order* (Chicago: University of Chicago Press, 1973), Chapter 2.

5. Ibid., Vol. 2: *The Mirage of Social Justice*, pp. 31–32.

6. Thomas Nagel, "The Meaning of Equality," *Washington University Law Quarterly*, Vol. 1979, p. 28.

7. Ibid., p. 27.

8. The book did not see the causes of these differences as cost-related, but this was pointed out in Walter E. Williams, "Why the Poor Pay More: An Alternative Explanation," *Social Science Quarterly*, Vol. 54, No. 2 (September 1973), pp. 372–379.

9. Milton and Rose Friedman, *Free to Choose*, p. 148.

10. Barbara J. Jordan and Elspeth D. Rostow, *The Great Society: A Twenty-Year Critique* (Austin: Lyndon Baines Johnson Library, 1986), p. 71.

11. John Rawls, *A Theory of Justice* (Cambridge, Mass.: Harvard University Press, 1971), p. 100.

12. Ibid., p. 275.

13. Jean H. Fetter, *Questions and Admissions: Reflections on 100,000 Admissions Decisions at Stanford* (Stanford: Stanford University Press, 1995), p. 45.

14. See, for example, John Kronholz, "As States End Racial Preferences, Pressure Rises To Drop SAT to Maintain Minority Enrollment," *Wall Street Journal*, February 12, 1998, p. A24; Nancy S. Cole, Educational Testing Service, "Merit and Opportunity: Testing and Higher Education at the Vortex," speech at the conference, New Direction in Assessment for Higher Education: Fairness, Access, Multiculturalism, and Equity (F.A.M.E.), New Orleans, Louisiana, March 6–7, 1997; Thomas Sowell, *Inside American Education: The Decline, the Deception, the Dogmas* (New York: The Free Press, 1993), pp. 122–126.

15. See, for example, Thomas Sowell, *Race and Culture: A World View* (New York: Basic Books, 1994), pp. 235–246; Thomas Sowell, *Migrations and Cultures: A World View* (New York: Basic Books, 1996), pp. 8–18; Thomas Sowell, *Conquests and Cultures: An International History* (New York: Basic Books, 1998), pp. 10–12, 99–109, 175–177, 205–207, 251–255, 347–348.

16. William G. Bowen and Derek Bowen, *The Shape of the River: Long-Term Consequences of Considering Race in College and University Admissions* (Princeton: Princeton University Press, 1998), p. v.

17. U.S. Bureau of the Census, "Marital Status and Living Arrangements: March 1992," *Current Population Reports*, Series P-20, No. 468 (Washington, D.C.: Government Printing Office, 1993), pp. 1, 2.

18. U.S. Bureau of the Census, *Historical Statistics of the United States: Colonial Times to 1957* (Washington, D.C.: U.S. Government Printing Office, 1961), p. 72.

19. See Ramsey Clark, *Crime in America: Observations on Its Nature, Causes, Prevention and Control* (New York: Simon & Schuster, 1970), pp. 319–320; *Miranda v. Ohio* 384 U.S. 436 (1966), at 472.

20. See, for example, William H. McNeill, *History of Western Civilization: A Handbook* (Chicago: University of Chicago Press, 1986), p. 45.

21. Elizabeth Wiskemann, *Czechs and Germans: A Study of the Struggle in the Historic Provinces of Bohemia and Moravia* (London: Oxford University Press, 1938), pp. 142, 148.

22. See, for example, Drew S. Days III, "Concealing Our Meaning from Ourselves: The Forgotten History of Discrimination," *Washington University Law University*, Vol. 1979, pp. 81–91; Margaret Bush Wilson, "Reflections on Discrimination in the Private Sector," Ibid., pp. 783–786.

23. Joel Glenn Brenner, "A Pattern of Bias in Mortgage Loans," *Washington Post*, June 6, 1993, p. A1.

24. Alicia H. Munnell, *Mortgage Lending in Boston: Interpreting HMDA Data*, Working Paper No. 92-7, October 1992, Federal Reserve Bank of Boston, pp. 2, 24, 25.

25. Bob Zelnick, *Backfire: A Reporter's Look at Affirmative Action* (Washington, D.C.: Regnery Publishing, Inc., 1996), p. 330.

26. *The Chronicle of Higher Education*, September 2, 1996, p. 22.

27. See, for example, Thomas Sowell, *The Vision of the Anointed: Self-Congratulation as a Basis for Social Policy* (New York: Basic Books, 1995), Chapter 3.

28. Jonathan Kaufman, "How Cambodians Came to Control California Doughnuts," *Wall Street Journal*, February 22, 1995, p. A1.

29. Olive and Sydney Checkland, *Industry and Ethos: Scotland 1832–1914* (Edinburgh: Edinburgh University Press, 1989), p. 173.

30. Robert F. Foerster, *The Italian Emigration of Our Times* (New York: Arno Press, 1969), p. 262.

31. Firdaus Hj. Abdullah, "Affirmative Action Policy in Malaysia: To

Restructure Society, to Eradicate Poverty," *Ethnic Studies Report,* Vol. XV, No. 2 (July 1997), p. 210. (Sri Lanka)

32. Jean Roche, *La Colonisation Allemande et le Rio Grande do Sul,* Paris: Institut des Hautes Études de L'Amérique Latine, 1959), pp. 388–389.

33. Roger P. Bartlett, *Human Capital: The Settlement of Foreigners in Russia, 1762–1804* (Cambridge: Cambridge University Press, 1979), p. 151.

34. L. H. Gann and Peter Duignan, *The Rulers of British Africa* (Stanford: Stanford University Press, 1978), p. 281.

35. Patricia E. Roy, "Protecting Their Pockets and Preserving Their Race: White Merchants and Oriental Competition," *Cities in the West: Papers of the Western Canadian Urban History Conference—University of Winnipeg, October 1974,* edited by A. R. McCormack and Ian MacPherson (Ottawa: National Museums of Canada, 1975), p. 115.

36. Andrew Tanzer, "The Bamboo Network," *Forbes,* July 18, 1994, pp. 138–145.

37. Ezra Mendelsohn, *The Jews of East Central Europe Between the World Wars* (Bloomington: Indiana University Press, 1983), pp. 23, 27, 99, 101.

38. An entirely different and longer list of large disparities appeared in my *The Vision of the Anointed* (New York: Basic Books, 1993), pp. 34–35. Other examples are documented in my *Conquests and Cultures* (New York: Basic Books, 1998), pp. 43, 124, 125, 168, 221–222; *Migrations and Cultures* (New York: Basic Books, 1996), pp. 4, 17, 30, 31, 118, 121, 122–123, 126, 130, 135, 152, 154, 157, 158, 162, 164, 167, 176, 177, 179, 182, 193, 196, 201, 211, 212, 213, 215, 224, 226, 251, 258, 264, 265, 275, 277, 278, 289, 290, 300, 305, 306, 310, 313, 314, 318, 320, 323–324, 337, 342, 345, 353–354, 354–355, 356, 358, 363, 366, 372–373. Extending the search for intergroup statistical disparities to the writings of others would of course increase the number of examples exponentially, even when leaving out those cases where discrimination might be a plausible cause of the disparities.

39. Greg Duncan et al., *Years of Poverty, Years of Plenty: The Changing Economic Fortunes of American Workers and Families* (Ann Arbor: University of Michigan Press, 1984). See also *Income Mobility and Economic Opportunity*, report prepared for Representative Richard K. Armey, Ranking Republican, Joint Economic Committee, June 1992, p. 5.

40. Americans with a net worth of a million dollars or more are just 3.5 percent of the population. See Thomas J. Stanley and William D. Danko, *The Millionaire Next Door: The Surprising Secrets of America's Wealthy* (Atlanta: Longstreet Press, 1996), p. 16. Moreover, even this figure may be unduly generous, since net worth includes many assets, such as household effects, which could never be turned into cash at anywhere near their purchase price.

41. Myron Weiner, *Sons of the Soil: Migration and Ethnic Conflict in India* (Princeton: Princeton University Press, 1978), p. 250.

42. John A. A. Ayoade, "Ethnic Management of the 1979 Nigerian Constitution," *Canadian Review of Studies in Nationalism*, Spring 1987, p. 127.

43. Daniel C. Thompson, *Private Black Colleges at the Crossroads* (Westport, Conn.: Greenwood Press, 1973), p. 88.

44. Donald L. Horowitz, *Ethnic Groups in Conflict* (Berkeley: University of California Press, 1985), p. 670.

45. Margaret A. Gibson, "Ethnicity and Schooling: West Indian Immigrants in the United States Virgin Islands," *Ethnic Groups*, Vol. 5, No. 3 (1983), pp. 190, 191, 192.

46. Helmut Schoeck, *Envy: A Theory of Social Behaviour* (Indianapolis: Liberty Press, 1966), p. 292.

47. Stephan Thernstrom and Abigail Thernstrom, *America in Black and White: One Nation, Indivisible* (New York: Simon & Schuster, 1997), pp. 184–188.

The Mirage of Equality

1. Herbert Stein and Murray Foss, *An Illustrated Guide to the American Economy* (Washington, D.C.: The AEI Press, 1992), pp. 8–9.

2. Robert Rector, "Poverty in U.S. is Exaggerated by Census," *Wall Street Journal,* September 25, 1990, p. A18.

3. Robert Rector, "The Myth of Widespread American Poverty," *The Heritage Foundation Backgrounder,* No. 1221, September 18, 1998, p. 1.

4. Thomas J. Stanley and William D. Danko, *The Millionaire Next Door: The Surprising Secrets of America's Wealthy* (Atlanta: Longstreet Press, 1996), p. 16.

5. Ibid., pp. 27–28.

6. Ibid., p. 113.

7. Ibid., p. 44.

8. Ibid., p. 33.

9. Ibid., p. 12.

10. Fernand Braudel, *A History of Civilizations,* translated by Richard Mayne (New York: The Penguin Press, 1994), p. 17.

11. Fernand Braudel, *The Mediterranean and the Mediterranean World in the Age of Philip II* (New York: Harper & Row, 1972), p. 34.

12. Duane Meyer, *The Highland Scots of North Carolina, 1732–1776* (Chapel Hill: University of North Carolina, 1961); "Scots," *The Australian People: An Encyclopedia of the Nation, Its People and Their Origins,* edited by James Jupp (North Ryde, N.S.W.: Angus & Robertson Publishers, 1988), pp. 762, 764, 765–769.

13. Robert C. Nichols, "Heredity, Environment, and School Achievement," *Measurement and Evaluation in Guidance,* Vol. 1, No. 2 (Summer 1968), p. 126.

14. Charles Murray, "IQ and Economic Success," *The Public Interest,* Summer 1997, pp. 21–35.

15. See, for example, Thomas Sowell, *Race and Culture: A World View* (New York: Basic Books, 1994), Chapter 6.

16. Bernard Shaw, *The Intelligent Woman's Guide to Socialism and Capitalism* (New York: Brentano's Publishers, 1928), p. 6.

17. R. H. Tawney, *Equality* (London: George Allen & Unwin, Ltd., 1931), pp. 24, 25, 28, 29.

18. Ronald Dworkin, *Taking Rights Seriously* (Cambridge, Mass.: Harvard University Press, 1980), p. 239.

19. Helmut Schoeck, *Envy: A Theory of Social Behaviour* (Indianapolis: Liberty Press, 1987), Chapter 4.

20. John Rawls, *A Theory of Justice* (Cambridge, Mass.: Harvard University Press, 1971), p. 78.

21. See, for examples, Helmut Schoeck, *Envy*, Chapter 8.

22. Michele A. Hernandez, *A Is for Admission: The Insider's Guide to Getting into the Ivy League and Other Top Colleges* (New York: Warner Books, 1997), pp. 117–118. See also pp. 3, 6, 7, 9, 50, 120.

23. Camilla Persson Benbow and Julian C. Stanley, "Inequity in Equity: How 'Equity' Can Lead to Inequity for High-Potential Students," *Psychology, Public Policy & Law*, Vol. 2, No. 2 (June 1996), p. 272.

24. Quoted in Lynne V. Cheney, "A Failing Grade for Clinton's National Standards," *Wall Street Journal*, September 29, 1997, p. A12.

25. Helmut Schoeck, *Envy*, p. 28.

26. See, for example, Thomas Sowell, *A Conflict of Visions* (New York: William Morrow, 1987), Chapter 6.

The Tyranny of Visions

1. Will Rogers, "On Preparedness," *A Will Rogers Treasury*, edited by Bryan B. Sterling and Frances N. Sterling (New York: Crown Publishers, Inc., 1982), p. 113.

2. Oswald Garrison Villard, "Issues and Men: Vested Interests," *The Nation*, January 16, 1935, p. 63.

3. Charles A. Beard, "The Big Navy Boys," *New Republic*, January 20, 1932, p. 258.

4. Bertrand Russell, *Which Way to Peace?* (London: Michael Joseph, Ltd., 1936), p. 199.

5. Quoted in Charles F. Howlett, *Troubled Philosopher: John Dewey and the Struggle for World Peace* (Port Washington, N.Y.: Kennikat Press, 1977), p. 134.

6. Paul Johnson, *Intellectuals* (New York: Harper & Row, 1988), p. 208.

7. Speech in the House of Commons, November 12, 1940, Winston Churchill, *Churchill Speaks: Winston S. Churchill in Peace and War*, edited by Robert Rhodes James (New York: Chelsea House, 1980), p. 734.

8. See, for examples, Thomas Sowell, *The Vision of the Anointed: Self-Congratulation as a Basis for Social Policy* (New York: Basic Books, 1995), pp. 3–5.

9. John Dewey, "Outlawing Peace by Discussing War," *New Republic*, May 16, 1928, p. 370.

10. Ibid.

11. John Dewey, "If War Were Outlawed," *New Republic*, April 25, 1923, p. 234.

12. Ibid., p. 235.

13. See, for example, Thomas Sowell, *A Conflict of Visions* (New York: William Morrow, 1987), Chapter 7.

14. John Dewey, *Human Nature and Conduct: An Introduction to Social Psychology* (New York: The Modern Library, 1957), pp. 18, 297.

15. Bertrand Russell, *Which Way to Peace?*, pp. 174, 176.

16. Ibid., p. 184.

17. Robert Shepherd, *A Class Divided: Appeasement and the Road to Munich, 1938* (London: Macmillan Co., Ltd., 1988), p. 50.

18. Winston S. Churchill, *The Second World War*, Vol I: *The Gathering Storm* (Boston: Houghton Mifflin, 1983), pp. 14, 413; Arthur Berriedale Keith, *Speeches and Documents on International Affairs: 1918–1937* (London: Oxford University Press, 1938), p. 49.

19. Winston S. Churchill, *The Gathering Storm*, p. 14.

20. Donald Kagan, *On the Causes of War and the Preservation of Peace* (New York: Doubleday, 1995), p. 314.

21. Bertrand Russell, *Which Way to Peace?*, pp. 146, 152.

22. Ibid., p. 343. Nor was this mere talk. The British Labour Party routinely voted against all military expenditures until the mid-1930s—when the ever more blatant threat of Hitler and a rapidly rearming Germany finally forced the party into mere abstentions on military votes in Parliament. This change, incidentally, was because of the non-anointed within the party—the labor union leaders, rather than the left-wing intelligentsia.

23. Oswald Garrison Villard, "We Militarize," *The Atlantic Monthly*, 1936, p. 144.

24. Norman Thomas, "What Will I Do When America Goes to War" *The Modern Monthly*, Vol. IX, No. 5 (September 1935), p. 265.

25. Gerald P. Nye, "Billions for 'Defense,'" *Forum*, Vol. XCV, No. 4 (April 1936), p. 208.

26. Neville Chamberlain, *In Search of Peace* (New York: G. P. Putnam's Sons, 1939), p. 192.

27. Ibid., p. 252.

28. Ibid., p. 45.

29. Bertrand Russell, *Which Way to Peace?*, p. 109.

30. Even war itself was recognized by Edmund Burke as not being something that required a justification by any prospective gains but was part of the price of preserving existing independence and freedom. Of those who asked what Britain was gaining by fighting France, he said: "They ask what they are to *get* by this war? Why! The wretches, they get their existence—they get the power of playing the fool with impunity by it—and is that nothing?" Edmund Burke, *The Correspondence of Edmund Burke*, edited by P. J. Marshall and John A. Woods (Cambridge: Cambridge University Press, 1968), Vol. VII, p. 416.

31. John F. Kennedy, *Why England Slept* (New York: Wilfred Funk, Inc., 1961), pp. 6–7.

32. An empirical study of the effects of gun-ownership by law-abiding citizens in the United States likewise showed that the spread of such gun-ownership was highly correlated with a *decline* in violent crimes. John R. Lott, Jr., *More Guns, Less Crime: Understanding Crime and Gun Control Laws* (Chicago: University of Chicago Press, 1998).

33. Dinesh D'Souza, *Ronald Reagan: How an Ordinary Man Became an Extraordinary Leader* (New York: The Free Press, 1997), p. 4.

34. Neville Chamberlain, *In Search of Peace*, p. 288.

35. Ibid., pp. 26, 27.

36. Ibid., p. 34.

37. Ibid., pp. 163, 179, 204.

38. Bertrand Russell, *Which Way to Peace?*, p. 205.

39. Winston Churchill, *Churchill Speaks*, p. 554.

40. Neville Chamberlain, *In Search of Peace*, p. 98.

41. Ibid., p. 133.

42. Ibid., p. 106.

43. Ibid., p. 5.

44. Ibid., p. 53.

45. Ibid, pp. 34, 40, 120, 209, 210, 216, 230, 240, 242, 250, 271.

46. See, for example, Edward N. Luttwak, "Churchill and Us," *Commentary*, Vol. 63, No. 6 (June 1977), pp. 44–49.

47. Winston Churchill, *Churchill Speaks*, p. 809.

48. William Manchester, *The Last Lion*, Vol. I: *Alone, 1932–1940* (Boston: Little, Brown and Co., 1988), p. 680.

49. Winston Churchill, *Churchill Speaks*, p. 884.

50. *Time*, May 14, 1945, p. 15.

51. James Bennet, "Between Wary Presidents, Signs of Bonding," *New York Times*, October 30, 1997, p. A1.

52. A fuller analysis of Marx's theories can be found in my *Marxism: Philosophy and Economics* (New York: William Morrow, 1985), especially Chapters 5–8.

53. Karl Marx and Frederick Engels, *Selected Correspondence: 1846–1985*, edited by Dona Torr (New York: International Publishers, 1942), pp. 115–116; Frederick Engels, *The Condition of the Working-Class in 1844* (London: George Allen & Unwin, Ltd., 1952), p. xiv.

54. Ibid., p. 63.

55. V. I. Lenin, *Imperialism: The Highest Stage of Capitalism* (New York: International Publishers, 1969), pp. 13–14.

56. Ibid., p. 29.

57. Ibid., p. 64.

58. Ibid., pp. 16–17, 18, 22–23, 31, 32, 38.

59. Ibid., pp. 64–65.

60. Mira Wilkins, *The History of Foreign Investment in the United States to 1914* (Cambridge, Mass.: Harvard University Press, 1989), p. 609.

61. Peter Mathias, *The First Industrial Nation: An Economic History of Britain 1700–1914*, second edition (London: Methuen, 1983), p. 300.

62. Ibid., p. 300.

63. Ibid., p. 107.

64. L. H. Gann, "Economic Development in Germany's African Empire, 1884–1914," *Colonialism in Africa 1870–1960*, Vol. IV, edited by Peter Duignan and L. H. Gann, p. 218.

65. L. H. Gann and Peter Duignanc, "Reflections on Imperialism and the Scramble for Africa," Ibid., Vol. I, p. 113.

66. U.S. Bureau of the Census, *Historical Statistics of the United States: From Colonial Times to 1870* (Washington; D.C.: Government Printing Office, 1975), p. 870.

67. Joseph A. Schumpeter, *History of Economic Analysis* (New York: Oxford University Press, 1954), p. 43n.

68. Jacob Riis, *How the Other Half Lives: Studies Among the Tenements of New York* (Cambridge, Mass.: Harvard University Press, 1970), p. 84.

69. Milton Friedman and Anna J. Schwartz, *A Monetary History of the United States: 1867–1960* (Princeton: Princeton University Press, 1963), pp. 495–496; Paul Johnson, *A History of the American People* (New York: Basic Books, 1998), pp. 752–759.

70. Benjamin A. Rogge, *Can Capitalism Survive?* (Indianapolis: Liberty Press, 1979), p. 110.

71. Peter Collier and David Horowitz, *Deconstructing the Left: From Vietnam to the Clinton Era* (Los Angeles: Second Thoughts Books, 1995), p. 12.

72. Adam Smith, *On the Nature and Causes of the Wealth of Nations* (New York: Modern Library, 1937), p. 16; F. A. Hayek, *The Collected Works of F. A. Hayek*, Vol. I: *The Fatal Conceit: The Errors of Socialism*, edited by W. W. Bartley III (Chicago: University of Chicago Press, 1988), p. 79.

73. F. A. Hayek, *The Road to Serfdom* (Chicago: University of Chicago Press, 1972), p. 137.

The Quiet Repeal of the American Revolution

1. Abraham Lincoln, "The Perpetuation of Our Political Institutions": Address Before the Young Men's Lyceum of Springfield, Illinois, January 27, 1838, *Abraham Lincoln: His Speeches and Writings*, edited by Roy P. Basler (New York: Kraus Reprint, 1981), p. 80.

2. Ibid., p. 82.

3. Ibid., p. 83.

4. Ibid., p. 83.

5. Curtis Sittenfeld, "Law Students Campaign for Rights of Prisoners," *The Stanford Daily*, November 7, 1995, p. 12.

6. Alexis de Tocqueville, *Democracy in America* (New York: Alfred A. Knopf, 1966), Vol. II, pp. 367–368.

7. The landmark case in the development of this doctrine was *Griggs v. Duke Power Co.*, 401 U.S. 424 (1971). An employment test that all job applicants at the Duke Power Company had to take was unanimously declared to be discriminatory against black applicants because a history of substandard education for blacks in the state's racially segregation schools made it predictable that they would fail such tests at a higher rate than whites. Duke Power's prior history of racial discrimination may well have suggested to the justices that this test was a subterfuge to continue that discrimination in an outwardly neutral guise.

8. Edmund Burke, *Reflections on the Revolution in France* (New York: Everyman's Library, 1967), p. 56.

9. James FitzJames Stephen, *Liberty, Equality, Fraternity* (Indianapolis: Liberty Fund, 1993), p. 170.

10. Margaret Bush Wilson, "Reflections on Discrimination in the Private Sector," *Washington University Law Quarterly*, Vol. 1979, p. 783.

11. Aristotle, "Rhetoric," *The Basic Works of Aristotle*, edited by Richard McKeon (New York: Random House, 1941), p. 1328.

12. Margaret Bush Wilson, "Reflections on Discrimination in the Private Sector," *Washington University Law Quarterly*, Vol. 1979, pp. 784, 785.

13. John Rawls, *A Theory of Justice* (Cambridge, Mass.: Harvard University Press, 1971), pp. 60, 61, 302.

14. Robin Wilson, "Yale Professor, a Unabomber Target, Takes Aim at Modern American Society," *The Chronicle of Higher Education*, September 19, 1997, p. A14.

15. "In the Malay States primary education in Malay was free for all Malay boys and gils, and compulsory for all boys living within a mile and a half of a Malay vernacular school. Estates employing over a certain number of Tamil labourers had to maintain a school and give free vernacular education to the children of Tamil labourers working on

the estate. There were no such facilities for Chinese." Victor Purcell, *The Overseas Chinese in Southeast Asia,* second edition (Kuala Lumpur: Oxford University Press, 1980), p. 277. Gordon P. Means, "Ethnic Preference Policies in Malaysia," *Ethnic Preference and Public Policy in Developing States,* edited by Neil Nevitte and Charles H. Kennedy (Boulder, Colo.: Lyne Rienner Publishers, Inc., 1986), p. 107.

16. R. Bayly Winder, "The Lebanese in West Africa," *Comparative Studies in Society and History,* Vol. 4 (1967), pp. 309–310.

17. See, for example, Thomas Sowell, *Preferential Policies: An International Perspective* (New York: William Morrow, 1990).

18. See, for example, Robert L. Schuettinger and Eamon F. Butler, *Forty Centuries of Wage and Price Controls: How Not to Fight Inflation* (Washington, D.C.: The Heritage Foundation, 1979); F. A. Hayek et al., *Rent Control: A Popular Paradox* (Vancouver, B.C.: The Fraser Institute, 1975).

19. See F. A. Hayek et al., *Rent Control;* Milton Friedman et al., *Rent Control: Myths and Realities* (Vancouver, B.C.: The Fraser Institute, 1981), William Tucker, "How Rent Control Drives Out Affordable Housing," *Policy Analysis* (Washington, D.C.: Cato Institute), No. 274 (May 21, 1997); Charles W. Baird, *Rent Control: The Perennial Folly* (Washington, D.C.: Cato Institute, 1980).

20. Mark D'Anastasio, "Soviet Health System, Despite Early Claims, Is Riddled by Failures," *Wall Street Journal,* August 18, 1997, p. A1; Cynthia Ramsay and Michael Walker, *Waiting Your Turn: Hospital Waiting Lists in Canada,* eighth edition (Vancouver, B.C.: The Fraser Institute, 1998).

21. Laurence H. Tribe, *Constitutional Choices* (Cambridge, Mass.: Harvard University Press, 1985), p. 187.

22. Aristotle, "Rhetoric," *The Basic Works of Aristotle,* edited by Richard McKeon (New York: Random House, 1941), p. 1326.

23. Anthony Lewis, "The Blackmun Legacy," *New York Times,* April 4, 1994, p. A13.

24. Robert H. Bork, *The Tempting of America: The Political Seduction of the Law* (New York: The Free Press, 1990), p. 6.

25. Oliver Wendell Holmes, *Collected Legal Papers* (New York: Peter Smith, 1952), p. 307.

26. *Kuhn v. Fairmont Coal Co.*, 215 U.S. 349, p. 372.

27. *Untermeyer v. Anderson*, 276 U.S. 440.

28. Letter of July 1, 1929, *The Mind and Faith of Justice Holmes: His Speeches, Essays, Letters and Judicial Opinions*, edited by Max Lerner (New York: The Modern Library, no date), p. 435.

29. Robert H. Bork, *The Tempting of America: The Political Seduction of the Law* (New York: The Free Press, 1990), p. 6.

30. *Samuel H. Moss, Inc. v. Federal Trade Commission*, 148 F.2d 378 (2d Cir.), cert. denied, 326 U.S. 734 (1945).

31. Ibid.

32. *The Borden Co.*, 62 F.T.C. 130 (1962), rev'd on other grounds, 339 F.2d 133 (5th Cir. 1964), rev'd 383 U.S. 637 (1966).

33. R. H. Tawney, *Equality* (London: George Allen & Unwin, Ltd., 1931), p. 229.

34. Ibid., p. 227.

35. Ibid., p. 234.

36. Computed from *The Baseball Encyclopedia*, ninth edition (New York: Macmillan Publishing Co., 1993), pp. 220–221, 249–250.

37. See, for example, the index category "Statistical Disparities" in Thomas Sowell, *Migrations and Cultures: A World View* (New York: Basic Books, 1996), p. 515.

38. *U.S. v. Lopez*, 514 U.S. 549 (1994)

39. Benjamin A. Rogge, *Can Capitalism Survive?* (Indianapolis: Liberty Press, 1979), p. 49.

Index